.... *jerome Rothenberg*

*The publisher gratefully acknowledges the generous contribution
to this book provided by the Literature in Translation Endowment Fund
of the University of California Press Associates, which is
supported by a major gift from Joan Palevsky.*

JOSÉ LEZAMA LIMA

SELECTIONS

JOSÉ LEZAMA LIMA

EDITED AND WITH AN INTRODUCTION BY

ERNESTO LIVON-GROSMAN

UNIVERSITY OF CALIFORNIA PRESS

Berkeley   Los Angeles   London

University of California Press

Berkeley and Los Angeles, California

University of California Press, Ltd.

London, England

© 2005 by the Regents of the University of California

Credits and acknowledgments for the poems and other texts included are on page 185.

All photographs reproduced in this book appear courtesy
of the Biblioteca Nacional José Martí. The photographers are unknown.

Library of Congress Cataloging-in-Publication Data

Lezama Lima, José.

[Selections. English. 2005]

José Lezama Lima : selections / edited
and with an introduction by Ernesto Livon-Grosman.

p.   cm. — (Poets for the millennium ; 4)

Includes bibliographical references.

ISBN 0-520-23475-8 (cloth : alk. paper).

ISBN 0-520-23476-6 (pbk. : alk. paper).

1. Lezama Lima, José — Translations into English.

I. Livon-Grosman, Ernesto.   II. Title.   III. Series.

PQ7389.L49A25   2005

861'.62 — dc22   2004044063

Manufactured in the United States of America

14   13   12   11   10   09   08   07   06   05

10   9   8   7   6   5   4   3   2   1

CONTENTS

DOCUMENTS

ACKNOWLEDGMENTS

I am indebted to a number of colleagues and friends who in different ways have contributed to the completion of this book. In Cuba: Eliades Acosta Matos and Araceli García Carranza from the Biblioteca Nacional José Martí; María Luisa Campuzano from Casa de las Américas; Reina María Rodriguez, Jorge Miralles, Antonio José Ponte, and Duanel Díaz Infante from Azoteas, all of whom made every possible resource and then some available to me. In the United States: Nina Gerassi-Navarro, Reinaldo Laddaga, Susana Haydu, and Roberto Tejada for their comments and engagement in detailed discussions about Lezama's work. A special thanks to series editors Jerry Rothenberg and Pierre Joris for their support and to Laura Cerruti from University of California Press for her attention to detail.

TRANSCENDING NATIONAL POETICS

A New Reading of José Lezama Lima

I

The first view of Havana immediately impresses upon a traveler the multilayered reality of Cuba. The multiplicity of political signs, whether they be the old pictures of Che Guevara or the newer bill-boards alluding to the forty years of the Revolution, are iconographic of Cuban reality, because in spite of their willingness to convey a message, Cubans disguise much more than they reveal. The visitor, no matter how informed beforehand about the intricacies of Cuban life, would very soon need to test and probably change his or her assumptions against what he or she sees and hears on Cuban news, from customers in coffee shops, in grocery stores, and through conversations with friends and intellectuals — some of whom are dedicated enough to read and think about the work of José Lezama Lima, by far one of the most complex figures of twentieth-century Cuban literature.

One of these assumptions is a certain didactic simplification of Lezama Lima as a one-dimensional figure: as the representative of the Revolution or its enemy; as the epic founder of a truly cosmopolitan literary magazine, *Orígenes,* or as the asthmatic patient who would stay home for long periods of his life and who almost never left the island or, after a certain point in his life, even his home. (Among the many photos of Lezama there is only one by now very rare set of pictures of him walking around Havana's Cathedral.) The complexity of his circumstances matches well the historical changes undergone by his country and ultimately by his poetics. It is this complexity, which Lezama himself refers to as "difficulty," that makes Lezama's work unique in an introspective sense and that also provides an opportunity to reflect on the extraordinary historical times in which it developed. Therefore we should look for the keys to his poetics not only in the texts themselves but also in their cultural settings and in Cuban society at large, so alive both before and after the Revolution.

In the opening statement of *La expresión americana* (1957), one of Lezama Lima's best-known books, the author declares: "Only difficulty is stimulating," a statement that has become Lezama's trademark, the departure point from which we are to approach his work in particular and, presumably, literature as a whole. The fact that, since Lezama's first exposure to a large Latin American readership in the late 1960s, his work has always been seen as difficult never constituted a real obstacle but rather an incentive for continuing to delve into it, based on an understanding that the complexity of his writing reflected his equally complex cosmogony. Lezama's poetic unveiling of reality is echoed in the complexities of the language itself. To recognize this serves as an effective strategy for questioning the cultural circumstances in which he was embedded without reducing them.

José Lezama Lima was born in Cuba on December 19, 1910, and with the exception of brief trips to Mexico in 1949 and to Jamaica in 1950, he spent most of his life in Havana, where he died in 1976. Yet his writing always went beyond the cultural boundaries of his nation. Lezama's private and public personas were barely separate, and many of his activities as publisher and cultural broker were marked by a noninstitutional, almost domestic, character. After the premature death of his father, when Lezama was only nine years old, he and his mother moved into his grandmother's house on Calle Prado and later to 162 Trocadero Street, where the writer lived until his death. His father's death left the family in a precarious situation from which the family never completely recovered. In spite of his family's financial difficulties and his own severe asthmatic condition, Lezama was able to establish around his home an expanding artistic circle of painters, musicians, and writers, which would become a defining factor of Cuba's twentieth-century cultural life. Lezama's work, his poetry,

Lezama Lima at a year and nine months old, 1912.

novels, and essays, are the result of the social and personal circumstances in which he developed his poetics, yet the facts of his life have proven so elusive that we still lack a comprehensive biography. Reading his work is, then, the best way of reconstructing his intellectual career, and with some limitations it provides a larger personal picture as well.

Restricted by his acute asthma and his financial situation, Lezama was housebound for extended periods. In spite of these obstacles he studied law in Havana and dedicated much of his youth to reading everything that came into his hands. Nothing went unnoticed; and many of those readings were to find their way back into his writing as more or less disguised rewritings. Lezama finished high school in 1928. In 1930 he became a law student, but the university closed down for political reasons, and Lezama spent the following years reading Góngora, Lautréamont, Valéry, Mallarmé, and Proust. It was during those years that he started to write essays and developed his own poetics and a network of friends and writers that later constituted his closest circle. In 1956 Lezama turned down a job teaching literature at the Universidad Central de Las Villas, but a year later he read a series of five lectures at the Centro de Altos Estudios that were published as *La expresión americana,* a collection of essays in which Lezama expressed his own encompassing view of Spanish American culture.

The Cuban Revolution took place in 1959, and in 1960 Lezama was designated director of the Department of Literature and Publications of the National Council of Culture. In 1961 he became one of the vice presidents of the UNEAC, the Artists and Writers Union of Cuba, and in that same year his two sisters left the island. Lezama, whose sometimes elusive public persona added to the complexity of his work, experienced the separations from his sisters as traumatic experiences that, like everything with Lezama, generated more writing, in this case in the form of extensive correspondence with them. Lezama's attitude toward the Cuban Revolution is a clear example of his elusiveness toward institutional life in general. Although he held an official post, and although he wrote a poem in memory of Che Guevara, it was never clear where he stood as a supporter of the Revolution.

In 1964 Lezama's mother died. In that same year he married María Luisa Bautista, his constant companion and the person who, during the last years of his life, helped him to cope with his increasingly deteriorating health. If we were to choose two determining moments in his career, instances that could be considered turning points of his life and work, they would be the editing of *Orígenes* and the publication of his first novel, *Paradiso,* in 1966. This novel granted Lezama the visibility both inside and outside Cuba that he truly deserved, a kind of recognition that he did not have before its publication. Although the ten years that separated the publication of *Paradiso* and his death were for the most part marked by health problems, they were also a time when his work was gaining an increasingly international appreciation.

In 1958 Cintio Vitier, one of the few members of the *Orígenes* circle still alive in Cuba, developed a massive history of Cuban poetry — *Lo cubano en la poesía* — in which among other things he canonized Lezama's writing in an effort to make his work and *Orígenes* organic components of Cuba's literary history. Since Lezama's death the number of works dedicated to his poetics has multiplied exponentially, as have the critical perspectives on his writings. These writers all had in common a desire to follow the multiple branching of Lezama's baroque poetics, as was the case with such canonical and esthetically diverse writers as Julio Cortázar, Severo Sarduy, Reinaldo Arenas, and Néstor Perlongher, among others, all of whom share Lezama's appreciation of the baroque imaginary.

2

Latin American literature has often been seen both inside and out of Spanish America as a dramatization of history, as a rehearsal, in content as well as form, of the cultural issues of the last five hundred years. This perspective is taken with the hope that a fresh realignment of major historical landmarks — the Spanish conquest, the wars of independence, the struggle for national organization, and so on — will provide the reader with a sense of continuity that directly or indirectly

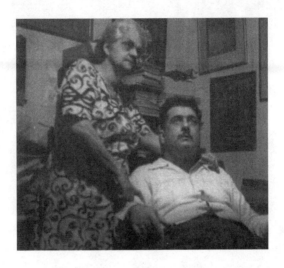

Lezama Lima with his mother, 1953.

answers the question, Who are the people alluded to in these books?
Or, How do we explain the present by recovering a sense of cause and
effect directly related to the past? Although for the most part very
helpful, this view tends to offer a series of chronological events, an
idea of progressive change and continuity that might create a sense of
identity and a homogeneous sense of history. Less frequently do we
find writers convinced that the most important Spanish American
cultural juncture was the dynamic fusion of indigenous, African, and
European influences — impossible to contain in a single definition of
identity or to fix in one historical moment — which saw its first day in
colonial times. Of course by definition such a vision cannot be reduced
to a single frame, either by form or content, yet Cuba's present culture
depends so much on issues of political independence.

It is enough to remember that while most of Spanish America de-
clared its independence from Spain between 1810 and 1824, Cuba was

Lezama Lima's *libreta universitaria,* 1936. This student identification "card" is a booklet and has a number of pages, three of which are reproduced here.

still a Spanish colony as late as July 1, 1898, when U.S. intervention ended the Spanish regime to replace it with its own occupation. The Cuban constitution of 1901, approved by Cubans and overwritten by the U.S. Congress that very year through the imposition of the Platt Amendment, gave the United States the power to overrule political, economic, and legislative decisions made by the Cuban government. In particular article 3 of the amendment, which represented American interests in the island, giving the United States the right to intervene for "the maintenance of a government adequate for the protection of life, property and individual liberties," curtailed Cuban sovereignty. This new colonial establishment put conditions on the evolution of the public sphere, which was left with very little autonomy, thereby delaying the formation of a cultural industry. The struggle to establish an effective government and a true separation from the United States was a political constant through most of Lezama's life.

From very early on, when he was a law student in the early 1930s, Lezama opposed the dictatorship of Gerardo Machado and later remembered with pride his participation in one of the largest student demonstrations of the time. Later he successfully navigated the fine line between his hope for the end of Fulgencio Batista's regime, which preceded the Revolution, and his equally personal ambivalence about associating his writing with institutional politics. However, in his poem "Thoughts in Havana," first published in *Orígenes* in 1944 and later included in *La fijeza* (1949), we hear an echo of political concern with the Americas as a continent, at the same time that Lezama makes a direct reference to the United States' intervention through his recurrent use of English (the italics in this translation by James Irby indicate the original lines in English):

> They want that death they have given us as a gift
> to be the source of our birth,
> and our obscure weaving and undoing
> to be remembered by the thread of the woman beset by suitors.
> We know that the canary and the parsley make a glory
> *and that the first flute was made from a stolen branch.*
>
> We go through ourselves
> and having stopped point out the urn and the doves
> engraved in the chosen air.
> We go through ourselves
> and the new surprise gives us our friends

and the birth of a dialectic:
while two dihedrals spin and nibble each other,
the water strolling through the canals of our bones
carries our body toward the calm flow
of the unnavigated land

Lezama calls on a common past; the verse "They want that death they
have given us as a gift" could be read as a reference to the United
States' intervention in Cuba's war of independence with Spain. They,
the carriers of the first flute, the one "made from a stolen branch," are
the Americas colonized by Europe, and both are by now inseparable
from each other. While Lezama is asking for an introspectiveness that
would give us friends, he also points out the existence of a dialectic
rift. The poem asks us to acknowledge the "two dihedrals," each of
them already forming a double angle, the North and the South, each
with its own geography, looking in turn at the indigenous as well as
the European components of their present, while we drift even fur-
ther into the "unnavigated land," a continental reality that presum-
ably will end the conflict between the two Americas.

As was the case with the Vietnam War for the United States, the
Cuban Revolution created for Latin America a dividing line, a before
and after, that changed the way Spanish American countries saw
themselves in relation to each other and to the rest of the world. The
Revolution not only inspired and supported many liberation move-
ments and multiple attempts to overthrow conservative or ineffective
Spanish American administrations, but it also promoted a pan–Latin
American movement based on the idea of a shared language and a
continental sense of cultural fusion, known in Spanish as *mestizaje*.
Although many of the issues included in the Cuban agenda, such as
land reform, nationalism, and the development of a national culture,
were already present in the Mexican Revolution of 1910, the conti-

nental, political juncture of the 1960s was marked by the search for a political model that could overturn the cultural and political dependency of Spanish American countries; this in turn created a common ground for a shared political project, making the Cuban Revolution an attractive role model. It was not — by any means — the first incarnation of a pan–Latin American proposal. Already during the wars of independence of the early 1800s Francisco Miranda had appealed to the British Crown, asking for support for a centralized Spanish American government with an Inca official as its head. Since then, the idea has been revisited and associated with a political model of diversity.

Lezama's own continental view of the Americas lacks any such explicit political ambition. Yet *La expresión americana* can at times be read as a precedent to the Revolution's model, and perhaps it even helped to negotiate his relation with the revolutionary establishment.[1] But like so many events associated with Lezama's work and poetics, the official reception of his work was uneven, and he lost official backing toward the end of his life. Lezama supported the Revolution and some of its ideals of justice and sovereignty, which of course were already upheld by his beloved José Martí, one of the most prolific Cuban intellectuals of the second half of the nineteenth century. Lezama'a attitude toward homosexuality created a similar effect to that of his politics. As if walking a tightrope, Lezama seems to have taken a guarded stance on these issues, not so much to hide his position but to avoid turning himself into a target. In this respect Lezama's position was not very different from that of so many other people at the time: on the one hand, sexual preferences were for the most part kept private, and on the other homosexuality was not exactly an open topic of conversation. Although in *Paradiso* he makes a direct reference to the homosexuality of some of its characters, Lezama's poetry, as well as the majority of his writings, doesn't. His marriage to María Luisa Bautista implied some sort of arrangement between them but was probably much more than just a cover-up: it was as much a good example of the complexity of Cuba's cultural life as it was a way of protecting her from future financial problems.

3

The evasive quality of Lezama's writing makes it quite difficult to bury his poetics under pre-established notions of national literatures or literary schools. Literary schools are aimed at creating, for the most part, a homogeneous, more general, picture in which the exceptions to the rules remain neatly on the margins. That said, it would be very difficult to introduce a selection of Lezama's work in translation without at least attempting an outline of some of those general historical circumstances that framed his poetics, even if only to stress his efforts to redefine the boundaries of some of these schools.

By now it is understood that what we call a national literature is always more than the sum of its parts. The works and their multiple branchings are in the long run far more important than any general claim in support of a group or an esthetic circle, which tends to be the rationale of national literary politics as we know it. It is quite common for the corpus of a national literature to escape the programmatic definition of a movement. In many cases whole periods of a national literature are cannibalized and reprocessed through the formulations of new genealogies — history as an effort toward active interpretation. In their own terms those new literary movements find and redefine their poetics in dialogue with their predecessors. Very early on, Lezama's poetics moved out of a restrictive national canon; and in a very inclusive way Lezama threaded his readings throughout his writing, using

Lezama Lima as a child in an army uniform, ca. 1916.

Spanish American, French, classical, and Spanish cultural icons to draw the contours of the fusion he thought of as Latin American culture.

What a work expresses, directly or indirectly, about national literature is always the tension between our insight about the writing itself and its context and potential for addressing the present. That is why our reading and its concomitant tension, in turn, change with each new generational reading, a transformation that in this case is due to the extraordinary richness of Lezama's work and his effort to challenge predictable expectations. Lezama's insistence on a baroque esthetic has come to be perceived for what it is: an invitation to the reader to take an active part and to rewrite as he or she reads along. Therefore a critical approach to Lezama's poetry in translation needs to take into account his poetics as well as its reception.

One of Lezama's distinctive intellectual hallmarks has always been the baroque, the Spanish as well as his own Spanish American version of it. A review of at least two general characteristics of the baroque is key to understanding Lezama's poetics. One is the way in which nature seems to extend or multiply itself in cultural products, as when Lezama fuses a botanical reference with a Renaissance painting, blurring the separation between culture and the natural world in another example of inclusiveness. The other is the tendency of the baroque to bare its internal conflicts and to thrive on them instead of smoothing them over. It is this tension that best explains the difficulty of his work, a difficulty that both challenges and seduces the intelligence of the reader. Lezama's work essentially asks for an active reader, one willing to immerse him- or herself in the intricacies of his images.

It is this kind of inclusiveness that made Lezama gravitate toward the Spanish poet Luis de Góngora and the seventeenth-century European baroque. The Spanish baroque in particular was at once an esthetic renovation, a critique of a decadent social system, and a powerful example of the impact of Catholic theology, all concepts that are well represented in Lezama's writing. Lezama's Catholicism constitutes a pillar of his esthetic, including the iconography of his poetry and the sublime tone of his writing. Take, for example, the opening lines of the "Sonnets to the Virgin," in which nature seems to reenact God's miracles:

Deipara, bearer of God! From such deceit
To ease his bulk of care, the cuckold sire
Saw need to separate both bird from wheat
And flower from bird, not being from desire.

The more we read Lezama's work the closer we get to realizing that his apparent obscurity is an invitation to the reader to get closer to the image-making process, as when Lezama proposes in "Fifes, Epiphany, Goats":

Clarities became dark. Until then darkness has been a diabolic sloth,
and clarity a contented insufficiency of the creature. Unchanged
dogmas, clear darkness, which the blood in spurts and in continuity
resolved, like the butterfly caressing the shepherd's forehead while
he sleeps. A birth that was before and after, before and after the
abysses, as if the birth of the Virgin were prior to the appearance
of the abysses. *Nondum eram abyssi et ego jam concepta eram.*

Lezama Lima and Salvador Gaztelu, 1931.

At times it seems that what really attracts Lezama to Catholicism is its mystery and that what attracts him to the idea of America is its darkness — "clear darkness" — the place where mystery multiplies.

Lezama's idea of America as the ultimate site for the baroque is neither a matter of continuity with the Spanish movement nor a search for a European genealogy. For him the Spanish baroque became fully developed in America because only there did it surpass a mere effect of accumulation or excess in gaining the kind of tension Lezama believed is created by the intersection of African, indigenous, and European cultures. In the poetry of Sor Juana Inés de la Cruz, as well as in the architecture of cities like Mexico City, Cuzco (Peru), and Minas (Brazil), the Latin American engagement with the Portuguese and Spanish baroque, with its extraordinary cultural fusion, is much more than a simple extension of the peninsular movement. For

Lezama, to write was to put into play a myriad of fragments, scraps of information, and cultural references, and his conception of the image depends on the tension that amalgamates those fragments. That cultural intersection forced Europeans, Africans, and locals to share symbolic space, creating, as I stated above, what we now call *mestizaje,* a vernacular culture that in Lezama's view, because of the fusion of its components, is a richer and more mature example of the baroque than is its Spanish counterpart.

In Lezama's writing difficulty is not a goal but a process, the result of his conception of the image, which — in turn — immerses the reader in a system constructed out of pure images, in many cases apparently divorced from an external referent. In fact, Lezama's complexity comes in part from his all-inclusive, sometimes encyclopedic system of quotes and references, which together with his very long and open grammatical structures contribute to his baroque style. Lezama sought and found a delicate balance between the Spanish influences that permeate, even today, everyday life in Cuba and the need for a truly Spanish American view of the arts. He rooted himself in the baroque, which he saw as the cultural bridge between the Spanish past and the American present — his favorite readings were Spanish baroque — and which was also in a new and unique way the fusion of the Spanish, African, and indigenous cultures. The repercussions of his poetics outlived him by several generations, and the neo-baroque brought back some of his esthetics, as with the writings of Severo Sarduy and Néstor Perlongher, both of them active explorers of Lezama's poetics.

Lezama's baroque legacy extended itself onto the next generation through writers like Severo Sarduy, who in turn developed a formal theory of the Latin American neo-baroque.[2] For Sarduy, as can be seen in his essay included in this volume, the Latin American baroque/neo-baroque is as much a way of writing as it is a way of reading. The neo-baroque has been disseminated beyond the boundaries of the movement, and its traces can now be found in the work of poets as different as José Kozer (Cuba), Gerardo Deniz (Mexico), and Haroldo de Campos (Brazil); it is less a literary school than an awareness, through linguistic expansiveness and bricolage, of the multilayered reality in which we live. In retrospect the neo-baroque was another way of proposing an inventive, experimental poetic practice that did not depend on the historical avant-garde. In fact, Lezama's kept an open connection with *modernismo*, the movement that preceded the historical avant-garde.

4

If the baroque is one of the threads Lezama wove through his work, then Spanish American *modernismo* is another. *Modernismo* — the Spanish American movement that in its own American way carried on a dialogue with French symbolism and was therefore quite different from what is called modernism — is for the most part associated with the late nineteenth and early twentieth centuries.[3] It was a movement dedicated, among other things, to building a bridge between the cultural legacy of Spain and the specificities of the Americas, in a continental sense. Though *modernismo* was well represented by several major poets from all over Latin America, one of them, Rubén Darío, became emblematic of the whole movement. Darío was born in Nicaragua but became, through traveling and holding various diplomatic posts, a truly continental figure and an effective promoter of the movement. That bridging came with a certain ambivalence, as can be seen in some of Darío's work, in particular "Salutación del optimista."[4] Darío thought that Spanish America's bright future was based in part on the newness of the place and its culture, as well as on the ties that connected it with a prestigious, European tradition.

As a movement *modernismo* strove to make clear that, in sync with political times, its poetics was the cultural product of those new nation-states, more American in a continental sense and more interested than ever in finding a vernacular register within its own writings. *Modernismo* was also concerned with retaining a link with a European cultural heritage that reached all the way back to Greek and Latin classical traditions and that sifted through Spanish literature and culture. This gesture, as foundational as the new political divisions that were reshaping the geopolitical map of Latin America, was possible only insofar as those "new" countries were politically independent, or, as they would prefer to call themselves, sovereign. For Lezama, who, after all, was born almost at the very peak of *modernismo* and whose country enjoyed such a late independence, the movement preserved a resonance that was already in decline in other Spanish American countries. Spanish American *modernismo* created a transitional place where new linguistic formations, that is, the continental vernacular, could be explored as a national language. At its best, adherents to *modernismo* explored the possibilities of contributing to the notion of national culture, knowing that the possibilities for foundational changes would remain open for a limited number of years.

Lezama's contribution was to explore those romantic elements already present in *modernismo* and to expand them in conjunction with a cultural political agenda that, by Spanish American standards, was quite unusual, given the history of Cuba's frustrated independence process. Not only did Cuba lack a cultural industry in the sense of a centralized book industry and mass-produced art forms, but at that time Cuba was also navigating a space in which it was still possible to go directly from being a colony to the true newness of being sovereign.

In comparison with other countries, Cuba achieved this transition from a Spanish colony to a revolutionary state much more directly than is the norm with the nation-state model so prevalent among most Latin American countries.

The extraordinary hybrid positioning of Lezama's poetry, his place in between *modernismo* and the avant-garde, was a direct and creative response to the transitional phase of the cultural institutions he was challenging. Noticing the experimental quality of his poetics is crucial because it reminds us that the meeting of explorative writing and the historical avant-garde is just one possible encounter. Experimental poetics like Lezama's have preceded the historical avant-garde and gone beyond the need for an organic connection with any given movement. It is only by taking into account Lezama's cultural context that we can start appreciating the complexity of his poetics. By responding to the cultural circumstances of his time, Lezama was able to create a new point of confluence by integrating anew all the components of vernacular culture.

Lezama Lima's work, canonical as it is, has been heavily read for his dedicated efforts to develop a foundational view of Latin American culture, a preoccupation that follows from his ever-present concern with origins. In this sense Lezama puts forward his own interest by exposing an all-encompassing project, while at the same time feeding a foundational equation: cultural fusion as continental identity. Any historical approach to his work will therefore need to take into account the circumstances and the cultural forces that made Lezama's work as well as *Orígenes* — the influential journal he edited from 1944 to 1956 — possible.

The development of his poetics, and, by extension, the work of the artists associated with his work, was directly linked to four literary journals, all edited or co-edited by Lezama. The first of those mag-

azines, *Verbum,* published only three is-
sues, all of them in 1937 — the same year
that Lezama published "Muerte de Nar-
ciso," his first major poem. The second
magazine, *Espuela de plata,* consisted of
six issues published between 1939 and
1941. A third one, produced in collabora-
tion with Angel Gaztelu, was called
Nadie Parecía and managed to publish its
tenth issue in 1944. The writers' use of
the journal as the preferred publishing
medium reflects a scarcity of distribution
means. In fact, the magazine format
proved to be the best way of establishing
a public space and of extending a writer's
social and intellectual circle.

It was also in 1944 that *Orígenes* ap-
peared for the first time, and it lasted
until 1956. Next Lezama published *La
expresión americana,* his most programmatic book of essays.[5] He co-ed-
ited *Orígenes* with the critic José Rodríguez Feo and relied on contri-
butions from a vast circle of Cuban intellectuals and artists: writers
Angel Gaztelu, Virgilio Piñera, Fina García Marruz, Lorenzo García
Vega, Justo Rodríguez Santo, and Eliseo Diego; painters Alfredo
Lozano and René Portocarrero; and musicians like José Ardévol and
Julián Orbón. For Lezama what best defined the dynamics of the
group was friendship, understood as an ongoing dialogue and as read-
ing one another's work, beyond the actual making of the magazine.
This particular quality, which could easily be overlooked, helps us to
understand that the relevance of *Orígenes* rests on the fact that so

Lezama Lima leaning against a
statue of Apollo in front of the
amphitheater, 1935.

The painter René Portocarrero, who was also a member
of *Orígenes*, and Lezama Lima, 1953.

much work was done with a fair amount of autonomy, with very in-
clusive editorial criteria, free from a rigid agenda, and always within
the dynamics of a social encounter. The center of all intellectual ex-
change was closer to the coffeehouse or to Lezama's home than it was
to a magazine office. Again, the social tissue, the sociability of every-
day Cuba, is key to assessing the impact and success of *Orígenes*.

Because of the historical proximity of Lezama's work and his im-
pact on the generation that succeeded him, his poetry was perceived
as the bridge in literary Cuba between the first and second half of the
twentieth century. In Spanish America this transition is much more
than a chronological passage through time; it also implicitly refers to
the transition from political independence to full-fledged nation-

A group at a cafe on Calle 23 and F, 1966. *From left to right:* Antón Arufat, Pablo Armando Fernández, Mariano Rodríguez, Lezama Lima, Heberto Padilla, Sigifredo Alvarez Conesa, Roberto Fernández Retamar, and Victor Casau.

state status. The avant-garde movements so present during the first half of the century were as deeply concerned with formal renovation as they were interested in reflecting on the present. *Orígenes* was interested in both, but Lezama would also make connections to other historical movements, rendering the journal a much more inclusive publication.

This perception — of *Orígenes* as an open, less programmatic journal — was framed by the fact that in the 1940s Lezama, as editor of *Orígenes,* engaged in a controversy with Jorge Mañach, the former editor of another Cuban literary magazine, the *Revista de Avance,* which stood for an avant-garde esthetics, one which equated progress with modernity. In retrospect, the exchange between these two editors is critical in understanding Lezama's poetics in a much wider context than that of the exchange itself.[6] The discussion, begun by Mañach through an open letter published in 1949, constituted a response to *La fijeza,* Lezama's book of poems from that same year. Mañach begins his letter by stating that *Orígenes* owes an intellectual debt to the *Revista de Avance,* because in his eyes the experimental character of Lezama's literary circle was simply a variation of his own avant-garde position. Lezama's response to Mañach's indictment was to create his own list of authorities, while asserting his own journal's merits in attracting a prestigious series of contributors. The list included the names of the writers published in *Orígenes,* such as Saint-John Perse, George Santayana, T. S. Eliot, and others whom, although not always included in the magazine, Lezama thought of as his group's equals: Alfonso Reyes in Mexico, and Ezequiel Martínez Estrada and Jorge Luis Borges in Argentina, all writers more concerned with rescuing tradition than with breaking away from it. If we compare the poetics of Lezama to those of Vicente Huidobro, the Chilean poet who founded *creacionismo,* one of the most visible avant-garde poetry movements in Spanish America, we will find that while *creacionismo* was trying very hard to break away from literary canons, Lezama was trying not only to include them all but in effect to expand them beyond the more programmatic avant-garde that in Mañach's view was associated with novelty and rupture from tradition.

Although the discussion between Lezama and Mañach offers us a sharper view of the positions at stake at a time when Cubans were openly discussing the possibilities of modernity, by focusing entirely on the opposition between *Avance* and *Orígenes* one runs the risk of distorting the picture by equating *Avance* with the only experimental agenda, while leaving *Orígenes* either in a more traditional position or in an indefinable critical space. In fact, recent critical readings of the

From left to right: Manuel Díaz Martínez, Roberto Branley, César López, Lezama Lima, Armando Alvarez Bravo, Fayad Jamís, and Onelio Jorge Cardoso, 1966.

work of some other *Orígenes* writers, such as Reinaldo Laddaga's work on Virgilio Piñera, José Antonio Ponte's essay on Lorenzo García Vega, and Duanel Díaz Infante's "Mañach or the Republic," successfully place *Orígenes* in a larger picture and offer a perspective from which to view both these magazines as part of the same tissue, while giving back to Lezama a much-deserved complexity. Although Virgilio Piñera was a prolific writer of poetry, short stories, and plays, his work has only recently started to be published again outside Cuba. Yet translations of his books into English are still rare. Like Piñera, García Vega was also part of *Orígenes,* and his extraordinary memoir of the group, *Los años de Orígenes,* published in Spanish in 1979 and already many years out of print, is indispensable in acquiring a deeper understanding of how so many different voices could be part of the

Lezama Lima in his study, 1960.

same magazine. Piñera and García Vega have remained for the most part invisible and in the good company, virtual as well as real, of other writers overshadowed by the Boom: Witold Gombrowicz, Felisberto Hernández, José Bianco, and Juan Rodolfo Wilcock, among others.[7]

Orígenes, not only the magazine but its circle of writers, would try to supply a unifying cultural model, thereby creating a sense of national identity — what Lezama likes to call in his "Colloquium with Juan Ramón Jiménez" a pure definition of poetry and, by extension, of culture, which I believe in Lezama's case is interchangeable with his poetics. For Lezama, a cultural blending is neither an ideal nor a goal, but a reality. Interestingly, his model of purity is anything but transparent and tends to set in motion an almost out-of-control mechanism of encyclopedic references that provide the content for his baroque sensibility. This attempt to create an all-encompassing Cuban poetics through *Orígenes* is paradoxical, given that the project did not follow an institutional model. This gap, between his vision of a unified, fusion model and the state of cultural institutions at the time, created the sense of displacement that even today we encounter every time we try to place Lezama's work in a larger historical frame. In this way Lezama's cultural project was several decades ahead of its time, and this fact in turn helps us to understand the late, but very positive, reception of his work by some of writers of the Boom, during the first years of the Revolution.

5

In spite of his work as a poet and editor Lezama was not very well known outside his country until the publication in 1967 of his first novel, *Paradiso,* which was received in the context of the international phenomenon known as the Latin American Boom. The young writers of the Boom — an ideological stance and a confluence of esthetic affinities more than an organic movement — were eager to distance themselves from the realism of the 1930s and 1940s, while preserving an interest in the social and the political. The core writers of the Boom — Gabriel García Márquez, Carlos Fuentes, Mario Vargas Llosa, and Julio Cortázar — who favored a monumentalist esthetic, which they thought capable of expressing the cultural complexity of Spanish America, saw in Lezama one of the greatest founding figures of their own poetics. Cortázar's efforts to promote *Paradiso* included one of the first and most influential critical articles ever dedicated to Lezama's work: "To Reach Lezama Lima," from 1967, included in this volume. Cortázar not only promoted Lezama's writing, but he also took upon himself the never-ending task of proofreading *Paradiso*. At least two aspects of Lezama's writing supported this genealogical, although retroactive, designation as a precursor to the Boom. For some of the Boom writers, Julio Cortázar and José Donoso among others, Lezama's work reformulated the Spanish baroque as a defining characteristic of Latin American identity, while integrating European, African, and indigenous colonial realities. In itself this reappropriation of colonial influence was a masterpiece of cultural fusion and offered a possible closure to the long-lasting discussion about the boundaries of Latin American culture, as well as to the formal and the content-oriented definition of those limits.[8] As part of his cosmogony, Lezama put forward a pan–Latin Americanism of sorts that was very much in tune with the dominant political agenda of the 1960s and 1970s, creating an extremely fertile climate for the reception of his work. A description of Lezama's unique situation as a writer, then, could start with the fact that in spite of his long, prolific life as a writer and cultural broker in his own right, Lezama's work was disseminated outside Cuba through, and to some extent was appropriated by, the eyes of the next generation, the Boom and its readers.[9] It is paradoxical that for many writers associated with the Boom one of the most obvious amalgamating factors of their generation was, without any doubt, the Cuban Revolution, which in turn would change forever the cultural environment in which Lezama established himself as a writer.

The association of Lezama's work with the Boom created a certain distortion in the reception of his work: while the Boom consisted almost exclusively of a group of novelists, at that time Lezama had published only one novel — *Paradiso* — and a few short stories, while the majority of his work consisted of an important collection of poetry and essays on poetics. Since the critical excitement generated by the Boom

Lezama Lima, 1975.

supported the idea of the novel as the ultimate genre, Lezama's poetry is often viewed as the path leading to his novels, the above-mentioned *Paradiso* and the unfinished and posthumous *Oppiano Licario*. Today, almost half a century after the first publications associated with the Boom, it is easier to look at Lezama's fiction, poetry, and essays as simultaneous, rather than as a precursor to exploring the same poetics.

If the continental projection of the Boom and the controversial exchange with Mañach over the avant-garde are clear ports of entry to Lezama's poetics, I would like to suggest another approach, that of examining one of his earliest essays. Lezama's interest in literary history was particularly evident in his efforts to formulate a theory of literature that would integrate Spanish and Cuban literary traditions into the same poetics. From very early on in his career this fusion can be seen, more indirectly in some of his first essays — "The Secret of Garcilaso" and "Sierpe of Don Luis de Góngora" — and more clearly in "Colloquium with Juan Ramón Jiménez" from 1937.

Lezama's "Colloquium with Juan Ramón Jiménez" constitutes one of the most spectacular acts of Euro-American ventriloquism of the first half of the century. The anecdote is simple. A famous Spanish poet, Juan Ramón Jiménez, visits Cuba and is courted by local writers. Lezama writes an entire dialogue between himself and Jiménez, writing both voices in a style that is so unmistakably his that Jiménez felt the need to write a short disclaimer published as an additon to the exchange: "I have preferred to accept everything my friend attributes to me and make it mine as much as possible than to question with a firm no as it is sometimes necessary to do with the attributed writings of others and easygoing talkers."[10] Lezama fulfills two goals. On the one hand, he pays tribute to an admired poet, and on the other he takes advantage of his fictional interlocutor in order "to talk" about Cuba with the impersonated distance of a foreigner. Earlier Lezama states "The crystal serpent is already on other skin and it takes us time to accept that the older skin is already paper, that paper falls with the elegance of a wrinkled leaf."[11]

In his introduction to the essay, Lezama suggests that the skin of the serpent is left behind, but the arrow that was covered by that skin moves on. It seems that at the time of his visit to Cuba Jiménez was that arrow, in a different skin. He has mutated while retaining the core, with that which does not change — that is, himself — serving as the perfect example of what he will be asked to discuss. Can Cuba be an island and still be Spanish? Is it just a change of skin? Does the place retain the arrow, or does it move beyond containment?

We now see that the main theme of this fictional, almost ironic, exchange arises from the question, Is Cuba an example of insularity? Or, more explicitly, Is it valid to speak of Cuban culture in terms of its distance from the European continent?[12] At one point, Jiménez, in the ventriloquist voice of Lezama, poses a question about the true consti-

Lezama Lima at his house, ca. 1970.

tution of an insular poetry. At the same time, "he" — Lezama through
Jiménez — says, "These days I have heard in Havana a lecture on
racial fusion, a fusion that would necessarily create a mestizo poetic
expression. I am interested in knowing if the search for a distinctive
insular sensibility is not the opposite of this mestizo expression."

To this, the "true" Lezama answers that artistic *mestizaje* implies
an unacceptable eclecticism, forcing poetry to choose between an ab-
solute love and a well-defined rancor, with nothing in between.

Furthermore, for Lezama, an insular sensibility is not in conflict with a universalistic solution. More important is for mestizo culture to imply a dissociation from a "feudal sensibility" and therefore a distancing from the kind of universalistic purity that Lezama sees as the destiny of every great national culture.[13]

In some ways this is the same cultural model that was dominant among the *modernistas*: the search for a form that would be their own not only because of its well-defined lines, but also because it would carry the original imprint of a new continent. If successful, this new form should attract a continental recognition.

The concept of a pan–Latin Americanism, as an all-encompassing cultural model, was not a novelty in Lezama's time. On the contrary, it is a cyclical cultural model that seems so appealing because it is almost a "natural" by-product of sharing the "same" language. Yet by the beginning of the twentieth century, that door was almost closed, and the boundaries that divided Spanish American countries had become sharper as a consequence of the nation-state formation. Lezama's work stems from his idea that the baroque quality of its images shares, in a sense, that continental quality that he thought of as a regained familiarity with the core of Latin American culture.

More than in his fiction or his essays it is in his poetry where Lezama's proposed tension between what we as readers are able to recognize as familiar and what we are out to discover achieves the highest intensity. In "Resistance" (1949), one of the prose poems included in this collection, Lezama, in ventriloquist fashion, explains what he does while he does it. The "resistance" of the title is already twofold: what we experience as readers while confronted with the text and what we should look for to reach an insight.

> What morphology allows, the realization of an epoch in a style, is very scant in comparison to the eternal resistance of what is not permissible.

Potency is merely the permission granted. Method: not even intuition, not even what Duns Scotus called confused abstract knowledge, reason in disarray. Method: not even creative vision, since total resistance prevents the organizations of the subject[. . . .] Then . . . *On this night, at the beginning of it, they saw fall from the sky a marvelous branch of fire into the sea, at a distance from them of four or five leagues* (Journal of Voyage, 15 September 1492). Let us not fall into the idea of paradise regained, for the men who came packed into a ship moving within a resistance could see a branch of fire fall into the sea because they felt the history of many in a single vision. Those are the times of salvation and their sign is a fiery resistance.

Our knowledge of the "permissible" is minimal in comparison to what we don't know and therefore should not be taken as a means of arriving at a safe harbor, but rather as an incentive to constant movement, even at the risk of dispersing and fragmenting that potency. For Lezama it carries more weight to propel the reader into his or her own series of associations than to reach a unique interpretation, a definitive meaning. The quote incorporated in the poem, indicated by the italics, is from Christopher Columbus's journal, the implication being that the founding of America was, for all parties involved, the product of multiple resistance. In Lezama's poetics resistance and difficulty are not merely preconceived by the writer but the result of a praxis of seeing and recognizing the poem as the tension between the images we as readers are acquainted with and the ones we are about to discover.

With the exception of Cintio Vitier, the other members of the *Orígenes* circle — Rodríguez Feo, Lorenzo García Vega, Virgilio Piñera, and René Portocarrero, among others — were less interested than Lezama in the creation of an autonomous critical system. For Lezama, the complex uniqueness of his poetics demanded a critical development but always as an extension of writing as a whole. At times this unique-

From left to right: Chiqui *(back to camera),* Lezama Lima, Roberto Fernández Retamar, José Bianco, María Luisa Bautista, and José Rodríguez Feo, 1968.

ness would create an equally distinctive hermeneutics and generate a dedicated body of criticism pointing to the singularity of Lezama's writing as inseparable from his literary persona. In this sense, Lezama resembles the American poet Charles Olson. Both were concerned with a foundational poetics capable of accounting for the originality of the Americas, and both in their own ways thought of continental migration in mythopoetic terms. Lezama, like Olson, was highly aware of the importance of place and he could say, like Maximus:

> I come back to the geography of it
> . . . .
> An American
> is a complex of occasions,
> themselves a geometry
> of spatial nature.[14]

Virgilio Piñera and Lezama Lima, 1968.

Lezama's Havana in 1910 was quite a different place from Olson's
Worcester, Massachusetts — except perhaps for the fact that both cities
are often defined by their connection to a colonial past. The differ-
ences prevailed, and Lezama's interest in American poetry never in-
cluded Olson or the Black Mountain writers with whom Olson was
associated. Nonetheless, both were very much aware not only of their
American condition but also of how much their America lay some-
where in between Europe and the indigenous cultures of this "new
geography." They shared the awareness that if European influences
were somehow a given, the same could not be said of the impact of the
indigenous cultures on the present Americas, that to recover what
colonial times have covered up so neatly would constitute an intellec-
tual challenge. Lezama saw it in the baroque quality of indigenous re-
ligious art, Olson looked for it in Mayan culture, and they both un-

derstood like few others that the newness of modernity was already embedded in America.

For the process of soliciting contributions from U.S. writers, *Orígenes* relied on Rodríguez Feo, the wealthy traveling journal editor. Lezama and Rodríguez Feo were very interested in T. S. Eliot and Wallace Stevens. Lezama felt an affinity with Eliot and Stevens both, being as they were concerned with the metaphysics of representation and the re-elaboration of European heritage. Like them, Lezama wanted to reinterpret and, to some extent, reinvent cultural ties with Europe. Lezama also shared with Eliot a rooted interest in Catholicism, an interest that shows more or less elusively in a good number of the poems selected for this anthology. But unlike Eliot or Stevens, he brought things European into his own idea of America, as he does when fusing the Spanish baroque and Afro-American tradition; and he merges them without the special effects of magic realism.[15] Lezama does simultaneously what very few others have done: he reviews the past with a strong sense of proximity, making tradition inseparable from the most alive aspects of the present. It is not a matter of nostalgia, as it is in the works of Eliot or Stevens, but of a baroque vibrancy that places him so close to Olson and Maximus. Ultimately Lezama and Olson shared a sense of fascination for the Americas as the ultimate, limitless place for intellectual self-discovery and invention.

6

Nothing really prepares us for Lezama's expansiveness, and therefore the work of translating these texts is as extraordinary as the original poems themselves. James Irby's and some of Roberto Tejada's translations were first published in *Sulfur,* while others were especially requested for this volume. Four of the seven translators included in this anthology worked on poems from different stages of Lezama's career, and they brought different assumptions about his poetry to the task. James Irby and Roberto Tejada managed to create a transparency that brings us right into the middle of the poem, creating the kind of enticement that we find in the Spanish texts. Gary Racz translated poems from one of the most baroque periods in Lezama's writing career, and his approach was to masterfully re-create the turns and obstacles of the original. Finally, Nathaniel Tarn's version of "An Obscure Meadow Lures Me" has the unique sound of twentieth-century American poetry, and, like the other translations, serves as an important reminder that the interest in Lezama's poetry has been very much present for a long time. The multiple translation strategies, as well as the variety of selections chosen for this volume, are meant to compose a complex picture offering the most precise possible view of the foreground with the best background definition. The creative and sustained work of the various translators involved in this project is one of the best keys we have today to Lezama's poetry. Since this is the first book-length anthology of José Lezama Lima's poetry in English, I have included poems from each of his books to show how Lezama's poetry slowly moves from the expansiveness of "Insular Night: Invisible Gardens" from *Enemigo Rumor* (1941) to the almost haikulike quality of certain stanzas in "They Slip through the Night" from *Fragments Drawn by Charm* (1977).

Lezama's poetics has remained faithful to its principles, almost as if time has led to a certain degree of compression, but now the images have also taken on an element of lightness. The images are still there, though in "They Slip through the Night" it is possible to see through them. The contours bear Lezama's style, but the center is truly full of unobtrusive specificity, as if proving that a concrete image can move further away from its referent, bringing us closer and closer to the re-

María Luisa and Lezama Lima, in one of the last pictures
of the poet, 1975.

ality of language. At the same time Lezama's poetics are important to
us because the issues that inspire his writing remain urgent, as we find
ourselves asking, once again, about the limits of national literatures
and cultures. His poetic plays on the tension between being inside and
outside national boundaries and between formal constraints and ex-
pansive content, and on the sometimes blurry distinctions between the
author and his writing, open up a dialogue with other works that we
now know reaches all the way to the present.

Ernesto Livon-Grosman
April 2004

NOTES

1 Lezama was not alone in his search for an all-encompassing view of the Americas. *Mexican Ulysses, an Autobiography* by José Vasconcelos, *In the American Grain* by William Carlos Williams, and *The Americas and Civilization* by Darcy Ribeiro are some examples of writings that reflect the sentiments found in Lezama's essay.

2 Sarduy's seminal essay "El barroco y el neobarroco," originally published in 1972, remains one of the clearest and most systematic on the subject (in *Obra completa*, 1999).

3 I use the term *modernismo* in Spanish to differentiate it from *modernism* in English. The former refers to a Spanish American literary movement that took place at the end of the nineteenth and the beginning of the twentieth century and was closely associated with French symbolism, while the latter is a term that is more broadly associated with post-symbolism and the historical avant-garde. In Latin America *modernismo* was chronologically followed by the historical avant-garde, and although some writers were associated with both movements at different points of their careers, it is fair to say that those involved in the avant-garde bore a strong desire to break away from *modernismo.*

4 Rubén Darío's 1905 "Salutación del optimista" is included in *Cantos de vida y esperanza* (in *Poesía*, 1977). For a long and comprehensive commentary on this poem and its ideological echoes, see Gerard Atching's *The Politics of Spanish American Modernismo.*

5 Lezama published forty issues of *Orígenes*, the last one in 1956, but it is not unusual to give 1957 as the last year of the magazine because, as Lezama himself stated in a conversation with José Prats Sariol and quoted in "La revista *Orígenes,*" "When we handed in the fortieth issue we weren't sure of the end." So perhaps we can say that 1957 was the year when *Orígenes* stopped functioning as an entity.

6 I am indebted to Emilio Bejel and his book *José Lezama Lima: Poeta de la imagen* (1994) for an insightful description of the exchange between Lezama and Mañach. A longer analysis of Mañach's poetics and intellectual biography can be found in "Mañach o la República" by Duanel Díaz Infante. This essay, to be published in Havana in 2004, was kindly lent to me in advance by the author shortly before I finished this introduction.

7   Witold Gombrowicz, who was stranded in Argentina during World War II with no job and very little knowledge of Spanish, nonetheless became one of the main influences on Argentine fiction writers who came after the Boom. While living in Buenos Aires he translated *Ferdidurke* from Polish into Spanish with the help of Virgilio Piñera, who was also living in Argentina at the time. The connection was more than circumstantial; they both shared an outsider's point of view that is embedded in their poetics.

8   Lezama developed his theory in *La expresión americana,* the five lectures he delivered in the Centro de Altos Estudios de la Habana in 1957.

9   One of the earliest and most daring assessments of Lezama's writing can be found in Julio Cortázar's article "To Reach Lezama Lima," included in *Around the Day in Eighty Worlds* (and this volume). During the first years of the Revolution this new valorization of Lezama's writing came mostly from outside Cuba. To better appreciate the complexity of his reception during those years it is worth looking at the criticism published in *Lunes de Revolución,* one the most reputable newspapers of those first revolutionary years.

10 "He preferido recoger todo lo que mi amigo me adjudica y hacerlo mío en lo posible, a protestarlo con un no firme, como es necesario hacer a veces con el supuesto escrito ajeno de otros y felices dialogadores" (*Obras completas,* 45).

11 "La serpiente de cristal está ya sobre otra piel y nosotros tardamos en convencernos de que la piel anterior es ya un papel, de que el papel cae con la elegancia con que se frunce la hoja" (*Obras completas,* 44).

12 The idea of insularity as a defining character of national literature can be found in the writings of other Lezama contemporaries from the Americas. Interestingly enough, only three years before Lezama's dialogue with Ramón Jiménez, Gertrude Stein delivered her *Lectures in America.* In one of them, "What is English Literature," she builds a case for the specificity of American literature by contrasting it to the particulars of writing in England: "On a continent even in small countries on a continent the daily life is of course a daily life but it is not held in within as it is on an island and that makes an enormous difference, and I am quite certain that even if you do not see it as the same anybody does see that this if it is the truth is the truth" (18). Lezama was far less inclined to claim this insular specificity and preferred instead to put Cuba on common ground with the rest of America.

13 My first encounter with the text was in Benigno Sánchez-Eppler's essay on Juan Ramón Jiménez and Lezama. His observations have helped me to shape my own ideas about Lezama's concern with the possibilities of an ongoing connection between Cuba and Spain.

14 *Maximus to Gloucester,* Letter 27 [withheld] (in *The Maximus Poems*, 184).

15 Lezama did not become associated with magic realism, although Alejo Carpentier, another baroque Cuban and a very influential novelist, was both a contemporary of Lezama and one of the founding fathers of that school.

KEY TO TRANSLATORS

TC   *Thomas Christensen*

JI   *James Irby*

SJL & CM   *Suzanne Jill Levine and Carol Maier*

GJR   *G. J. Racz*

NT   *Nathaniel Tarn*

RT   *Roberto Tejada*

POEMS

.

AN OBSCURE MEADOW LURES ME

An obscure meadow lures me,
her fast, close-fitting lawns
revolve in me, sleep on my balcony.
They rule her reaches, her indefinite
alabaster dome re-creates itself.
On the waters of a mirror,
the voice cut short crossing a hundred paths,
my memory prepares surprise:
fallow deer in the sky, dew, sudden flash.
Without hearing I'm called:
I slowly enter the meadow,
proudly consumed in a new labyrinth.
Illustrious remains:
a hundred heads, bugles, a thousand shows
baring their sky, their silent sunflower.
Strange the surprise in that sky
where unwillingly footfalls turn
and voices swell in its pregnant center.
An obscure meadow goes by.
Between the two, wind or thin paper,

the wind, the wounded wind of this death,
this magic death, one and dismissed.
A bird, another bird, no longer trembles.

• N T •

INSULAR NIGHT:
INVISIBLE GARDENS

Sleek and divided, a whippet twice-over
the moment it scatters its sweet assault,
its extremities, rings and fragments,
striding, they're disobedient,
enemies to time.
Green nerve of it reeling
in the most transient season of dew
that keeps the dark coffer of crystals
a secret from its body.
Out of slumber the balmy world stretches
its immaculate assault,
and numbered men, sweetly groomed,
on clouds, are as furious
as animals in ruinous packs.

Multiplied in summer,
rose-colored myriads of windows
fail to sweeten, pose no question, enamor no one,
nor do possible dreams of it sanctify
the swollen numbers, hippogriffs

that cradle somnambulant scissors to sleep,
long white locks of guitars,
horses that the rain girdles
with concise keys and soft flames.

Slow and masterful, a window to the blaze,
in the blindest expanse of the empire,
reappears playing the otherwordly game
of sandlike timbres out of jars.
The rich fabric of its grief
is unable to make chimes swell,
and its hard tenacity, a tent
bearing grotesque signs of exile,
like a statue down a river floating,
dissolving away, blindly carving
or deriding its debts to glory.
A falcon undissuaded by water
spreads its yellow ices,
a suddenly awakened murmur
like dewdrops erasing footmarks
and that amplify the sign language
of boredom, anger, and disdain.
The sobriety of riffled water fitting,
its passions outrivaling any leisure.
Swash of it splashing on the rooftop
of a sinister mansion riddled with holes.

Offering the breeze its tournaments
the falcon removes the oblation from its flame,
its yellow ices.
Secret garden speechless

where a sign begins its frenzy.
O circumspect, my goddess of the sea,
abandon your quiet caves,
rain in every cave your silences
the snow melts as gently
as a flower assailed by sleep.
O broken flower, disconsolate flake,
foldings of the slowest crackle
in the troubled passion of your worlds
stay as a shadow to the abandoned
body that is forever entertained
between river and echo.

Green flare-conveying insects
vanish in the voracious silent beacon.
In throbbing silences, in errant
spirals of cinder and mire, ashes
are defeated, damsels of rancor made
dim, surrendered softly
into scales and a forehead caressed.
As-yet existing ivory dignifies
fatigue like the black squares
of a weightless sky.
A buck's eternal slenderness
blares invisible flutes
like an insect grimed green-gold.
With limbs unencumbered
water reasons around simple rocks,
and joins the sinister smoke
that spreads without a sound.

Bitter manchild, O damsel-circumspect,
in the familiar wetness of your gardens
transformed into a hart the lad
who pulled up flowers nightly with
his scales set to weigh nocturnal water.
His howl an enveloping frost.
You, the seducer, irate dog
of a low interwoven flame,
canine of flames and damnation,
around snowy rocks and foreheads
in green-black vexation, mellow sauntering.
Drop by slow sweet drop
skin oozes in smoldering flurries.

The same minutiae of light
forebodes the farthest faces.
Light will arrive braided and meek,
air reminded barely of water.
Purveyor still devoid of agile sword.
Brevity of this light, supreme finesse.
In your palaces of billowing domes,
gardens and the steamy orchestra of their weight
inhale with the eiderdown of painted travelers.
Lost in seaside cities
horses sigh in caressed definitions
blind conveyors of lemons and mussels.
Night finds no place to rattle the strings
of your purple violins.
Inadvertent clouds and invisible men,
gardens slowly commencing

the frail nightingale threading carbuncles
of the siesta pressed ajar
and the idle river of death.

The violet sea longs for the birth of gods,
for to be born here is an unspeakable feast,
a drumroll of commanding retinues and tritons.
Motionless sea and birdless air,
sweet horror of the city's birth
scarcely remembered.
Grapes and the nautilus of somber writing
contemplate a chain of prisoners,
the sinister limits of their gait,
ephebes painted in their distant patter,
gloomy angels following their flutes,
briefly resounding their chains.

Enter naked into your marble beds.
Live and recollect like the painted travelers,
revolving cities, green-black liquid gardens,
enveloping violet sea, arrested light,
supreme finesse, the amusing buoyant air,
like animals out of irreplaceable sleep,
or, like an angelic rider of light, do you
prefer to inhabit the bounding song
of the unauthored cloud that swims in the looking glass
   or the invisible face that dwells between the comb and lake?

Welcome light,
pervader of burnished bodies,
glass fortified by fire,

sending its pleasant measures of dew.
In these balmy worlds, men prolong jasmine,
yawn clouds, stretching like dewdrops
out of which horses charge.
When not otherwise ordaining, the gods forget,
they separate the dewdrops from the waning green.
But the venerable and final night
safekept the tugged fish, its agony
of carmine barbs,
like a seafarer marked by downy ashes
and roseate conceit.

Sallied forth among reeds of glass
or sunflowers, their sky diminishes,
its tongue pointed at
encrypted canaries and antelopes,
with honeyed marks and exhorted neck.
Its transient behavior guilded again
by collections of strawberries that thirst,
porcelain or bamboo, gesture of a gloating
crane, bird-flame, reseda,
misted bird, briefly rock-a-byed.
Lacquered gardens bound
by the sky that paints
what the hand gently erases.
Noble measure of time by caresses.
In a slumbering timbre the hours fluttered
enfolded by doves and by sand.

Caressed by that eternal moss,
the supple hips of a gentle ebb and flow

are governed by the distant planet
with its attendant silver breathing.
A resounding voice arises in the chorus.
Let nymphs braid death and grace together
like tiny dewdrops offered to the god.
Let light dance disguising its face.
And let nightfall and flutes return
parceling their smiles in the air.
A commencement of cymbals expelling
dark animals with drizzled brows;
to the inexpressive, falsifying night
lewd animals seated on the rock,
lusty candelabras and horns
made of guilty metal and flitted sounds.
Banishing the fissured emissary arch
sound's transparency deceases.
Flutes' green-gold fractures
interlocking antelopes of corpulent snow
and abbreviated bounds tormenting the cloud.
Can an outbreak of hailstones in the dream
question the cloud or face
in pursuit of its wounds?
Let light dance reconciling
men to their disdainful gods.
Each, smiling, tells
the conquests of universal death
and the unruffled property of light.

· R T ·

A BRIDGE,
A REMARKABLE BRIDGE

In between waters frozen or boiling,
a bridge, a remarkable bridge that's hidden,
but it spans over its own handwritten manuscript,
over its own suspicion of its ability to pilfer
parasols from pregnant women,
with pregnancy of a question conveyed on the back of a mule
impelled to accomplish the mission
that is to elongate or alter gardens into alcoves
where children lend their curls to waves,
because waves are as mannered as God's yawning,
like the games of gods,
like the nautilus covering a village
with its dice-thrown, half-scored
inflection, and of animals crossing
the bridge with the latest Edison
safety bulb. The lightbulb, happily,
blows out, and onto the other side of the worker's face,
I entertain myself by placing pins,
for he was one of my loveliest friends
and I secretly envied him.

A bridge, a remarkable bridge that's hidden,
bridge that was a byway for drunks
who claimed they required a diet of cement,
while, lion-hearted, the poor cement
surrendered its riches as depicted by a miniaturist
because, mind you, on Thursdays, bridges
busy themselves as crossings for deposed kings
unable to forget the last chess game played
between a whippet whose microcephalia is reiterated
and a great wall that crumbles
like a cow's skeleton
seen through a skylight, geometrical and Mediterranean.
Led by astronomical numbers of ants
and by a camel made of smoke, a great silver shark
must now cross the bridge,
in point of fact it's only three million ants
that in a momentous hernia-producing buoy
lift the silver shark at midnight
across the bridge as if it were another ousted king.

A bridge, a remarkable bridge, hence it's hidden,
honey-colored armature, maybe it's the Sicilian vespers
painted on a small poster
painted also with a great crash of water
when it all ends in the saline silver
we have to cross despite the silent swollen
armies that have laid siege to the city without silence
because they know I'm there
and I saunter and I see my wounded head
and the immutable squadrons exclaim:

It's a beating drum,
We lost my fiancée's favorite flag,
I'd like tonight to drift into sleep poking holes in my sheets.
Remarkable bridge, my mind's matter,
and the drumrolls nearing closer to home,
thereafter I don't know what happened, but it's midnight now,
and I'm crossing what my heart feels is a remarkable bridge.
But the back of the remarkable bridge can't hear what I'm saying:
that I was never able to feel hunger
for since I was blinded
I've placed in the middle of my bedroom
a great silver shark
from which, meticulously, I break off pieces
I roll into the shape of a flute
that the rain amuses, defines, and congregates.
But my nostalgia is endless,
because such nourishment endures a stern eternity,
and it's likely hunger and jealousy
can only replace the great silver shark
I've set at the center of my room.
But no hunger, no jealousy, not this animal,
a favorite of Lautréamont, ought to cross alone and conceited
over the remarkable bridge, because the goats of noble Hellenic
    descent
displayed their flute collection at the last international
exhibit, of which today an echo lingers
in the nostalgic morning prone to pilgrimage, when the sea's torso
gives way to a small green bedspread and verifies its cabinet
of pipes, where so many bats have been set aflame.

Carolingian roses burgeoned on the edge of a crooked rod.
In the fourth quarter of midnight, a cone of water
formed by mules sepulchered in my garden reveals
that the bridge wants to fashion such exquisite belongings.
Little hands of ancient idols, absinthe infused with the rapture
of high-soaring birds that mollify the part of the bridge
supported over squashy cement, almost jellyfish-like.

But now to salvage my head it's time
for metallic tools to be stunned mirroring
the danger of drool now shaped into shellfish glazed
by the acid of unpardonable kisses
the morning tucks into a new change purse.
Does the bridge, turning, only envelop
the mistletoe and its olive-colored tenderness,
or around the hump and scratched violin
that grates the side of the leaking bridge?
And morning's campana can't even transform
the pink flesh of the unforgetting mollusk
into dental notches of the glazed shellfish.
Remarkable bridge, unbridled bridge
that nuzzles boiling waters,
and sleep an onslaught to the flesh until it's rendered soft
and the edge of unexpected moons resounds to the end with
    mermaids
oozing their latest seaside proclivity.
A bridge, a remarkable bridge, it's hidden,
waters boiling, frozen, surging
against the last defensive wall

to ravish the mind, the single voice
crosses the bridge again, like the blind king
who, unbeknownst to him, has been deposed,
and he dies mended tenderly to the allegiance of night.

· R T ·

SONNETS TO THE VIRGIN

I

Deipara, bearer of God! From such deceit
To ease his bulk of care, the cuckold sire
Saw need to separate both bird from wheat
And flower from bird, not being from desire.

So let the mill, God-bearer, be what will phase
Out man's coarse being, a break with life entire.
The shadow turns with bulk no one should praise,
Nor ugliness, nor millions who admire.

Hear! You, unmeasured, wish not to create.
Still, sleeping and awake, you've heard the dried
Wheat, the sistrum, the angel's trumpet blare,

The snow that blankets forests with its weight.
You've felt eternal life stir in your side
And laid to rest that star of strident glare.

*Mais tes mains (dit l'ange à Marie) sont merveilleusement
bénies. Je suis le jour, je suis la rosée; mais toi, tu est l'Arbre.*
— Rainer Maria Rilke, *Vie de Marie*

The stamp of clear resemblance still in place,
The cloud, as in the hollow space of towers,
Now crosses paths with blessedness and grace.
Oh faithful woman, dream of glass that shines

Its own pure dew, sure tree all may embrace,
The Unbeliever's opposite — his hours
Find spiraling ascents, misfortune's face,
A pyre of groans, a word that flees in time.

To tumble down your lofty crown's fair glow,
The angels all remain in place or hide,
Since you've paid heed to light brought here below

By just that lamb this very light unveils
To offer whiteness to the fallen snow
And spread snow where the lamb will forge his trails.

| | |

A captive tanglement lurks in your side,
A snow-white feather quill that wounds the throat.
The brief throne and its throneless moment bide
Time trembling at the humming's rising note.

Not shadow or mere infant, sleep denied,
Among us heaven's armature lets float

Its soundless aria's and pale son's stride
Against the wind, a duped and ruffled boat.

The wall of dream falls slowly to the ground,
Sweet custom of an unsure time's ill ease;
A shout lays low its ladder's bracing truss.

The wind guides a new vessel o'er the seas
While shadows seek what owners might be found.
What if we die and wings don't come to us?

IV

Still, you will come; it's you there I perceive
Amid waves of a mantle ne'er undone,
Inviting me to what I fast believe:
My Paradise, your Word — incarnate one.

Confined within a wicker basket's weave
Or climbing up high cherry boughs for fun;
Such wakeful passage makes what's ugly leave,
Become the face of your Beloved Son.

The pin will bathe itself inside the rose,
Whose smell and meaning turn, then, into dream,
Oppressive air the horseman jostles free.

The tree will lower down exquisite prose
And death cease being sound in the extreme.
Your shadow will cut short eternity.

· GJR ·

SUMMONS OF THE DESIRER

Full of desire is the man who flees from his mother.
To take leave is to raise a dew for civil marriage with the saliva.
The depth of desire is not measured by the expropriation of
  the fruit.
Desire is to cease from seeing one's mother.
It is the uneventfulness of day which prolongs itself
and it is night that such absence goes driving down into like a knife.
In this absence a tower opens, in that tower a hollow fire dances.
And thus it widens out and the absence of the mother is a sea at rest.
But the fugitive fails to see the questioning knife:
it is from the mother, the shuttered windows, that he is escaping.
What has gone down into old blood sounds empty.
The blood is cold when it goes down and is far-flung in circulation.
The mother is cold and has served her time.
If death is responsible, the weight is doubled and we are not set free.
It is not through the doors where our own loss looks out.
It's in the clearing, through which the mother keeps on walking but
  no longer follows us now.
It's through a clearing: there she blinds herself and leaves us well.

Alas for him who walks that path no longer where the mother no
   longer follows him, alas.
It is not self-ignorance, self-knowledge continues to rage as in
   her time,
but to follow it would be to burn *à deux* in a tree,
and she hungers to clap eyes on the tree like a stone,
a stone inscribed with the rules of ancient games.
Our desire is not to overtake or incorporate a bitter fruition.
Full of desire is the fugitive
and from our head-on collision with our mothers falls the
   centerpiece planet
and from where do we flee, if it is not from our mothers that we flee,
that never wish to play these cards again, go through the night
   again, the night of such unearthly suffering in the sides?

· NT ·

THOUGHTS IN HAVANA

Because I dwell in a whisper like a set of sails,
a land where ice is a reminiscence,
fire cannot hoist a bird
and burn it in a conversation calm in style.
Though that style doesn't dictate to me a sob
and a tenuous hop lets me live in bad humor,
I will not recognize the useless movement
of a mask floating where I cannot,
where I cannot transport the stonecutter or the door latch
to the museums where murders are papered
while the judges point out the squirrel
that straightens its stockings with its tail.
If a previous style shakes the tree,
it decides the sob of two hairs and exclaims:
mi alma no está en un cenicero.

Any memory that is transported,
received like a galantine from the obese ambassadors of old,
will not make us live like the broken chair
of the lonesome existence that notes the tide

and sneezes in autumn.
And the size of a loud laugh,
broken by saying that its memories are remembered,
and its styles the fragments of a serpent
that we want to solder together
without worrying about the intensity of its eyes.
If someone reminds us that our styles
are already remembered;
that through our nostrils no subtle air thinks forth
but rather that the Aeolus of the sources elaborated
by those who decided that being
should dwell in man,
without any of us
dropping the saliva of a danceable decision,
though we presume like other men
that our nostrils expel a subtle air.
Since they dream of humiliating us,
repeating day and night with the rhythm of the tortoise
that conceals time on its back:
you didn't decide that being should dwell in man;
your God is the moon
watching like a banister
the entrance of being into man.
Since they want to humiliate us we say to them:
el jefe de la tribu descendió la escalinata.

They have some show windows and wear some shoes.
In those show windows they alternate the mannequin with the
    stuffed ossifrage,

and everything that has passed through the forehead
of the lonesome buffalo's boredom.
If we don't look at the show window, they chat
about our insufficient nakedness that isn't worth a figurine from
    Naples.
If we go through it and don't break the glass,
they don't stress amusingly that our boredom can break the fire
and they talk to us about the living model and the parable of the
    ossifrage.
They who carry their mannequins to all the ports
and who push down into their trunks a screeching
of stuffed vultures.
They don't want to know that we climb up along the damp roots of
    the fern
— where there are two men in front of a table; to the right, the jug
and the bread that has been caressed — ,
and that though we may chew their style,
no escogemos nuestros zapatos en una vitrina.

The horse neighs when there's a shape
that comes in between like a toy ox,
that keeps the river from hitting it on the side
and kissing the spurs that were a present
from a rosy-cheeked adulteress from New York.
The horse doesn't neigh at night;
the crystals it exhales through its nose,
a warm frost, of paper;
the digestion of the spurs
after going through its muscles now glassy

with the sweat of a frying pan.
The toy ox and the horse
hear the violin, but the fruit doesn't fall
squashed on their backs that are rubbed
with a syrup that is never tar.
The horse slides over the moss
where there is a table exhibiting the spurs,
but the perked-up ear of the beast doesn't decipher.

The calm with stumble music
and drunken circus horses in a tangle,
where the needle bites because there's no leopard
and the surge of the accordion
elaborates some tights of worn taffeta.
Though the man doesn't leap, there's a sound
of divided shapes in each indivisible season,
because the violin leaps like an eye.
The motionless jugs stir up a cartilaginous echo:
the shepherd's blue belly
is displayed on a tray of oysters.
In that echo of the bone and the flesh, some snorts
come out covered with a spiderweb disguise,
for the delight to which a mouth is opened,
like the bamboo flute elaborated
by the boys always asking for something.
They ask for a hollow darkness
to sleep in, splitting open, with no sensitivity,
the style of their mothers' bellies.
But while they sharpen a spiderweb sigh

inside a jug passing from hand to hand,
the scratch on the lute doesn't decipher.
He indicated some moldings
that my flesh preferred to almonds.
Some delicious moldings riddled with holes
by the hand that wraps them
and sprinkles them with the insects that will accompany it.
And that waiting, waited for in the wood
by its absorption that doesn't stop the horseman,
while not some masks, the ax cuts
that do not reach the moldings,
which do not wait like an ax or a mask,
but like the man who waits in a house of leaves.
But in tracing the cracks in the molding
and making a glory of the parsley and the canary,
l'étranger nous demande le garçon maudit.

The musk ox itself knew the entrance,
the thread of three secrets
continued till it reached the terrace
without seeing the burning of the grotesque palace.
Does a door collapse because the drunken man
with no boots on yields to it his dream?
A muddy sweat fell from the shafts
and the columns crumbled in a sigh
that scattered their stones as far as the brook.
The roofs and the barges
safeguard the calm liquid and the chosen air;
the roofs that are friends of the toy tops
and the barges that anchor in a truncated backland,

scatter in confusion caused by a stuffed gallantry that catches
    unawares
the weaving and the obverse of the eye shivering together in masks.

To think that some crossbowmen
shoot at a funeral urn
and that from the urn leap
some pale people singing,
because our memories are already remembered
and we ruminate with a very bewildered dignity
some moldings that came out of the hunter's pecked siesta.
To know whether the song is ours or the night's,
they want to give us an ax elaborated in the sources of Aeolus.
They want us to leap from that urn
and they also want to see us naked.
They want that death they have given us as a gift
to be the source of our birth,
and our obscure weaving and undoing
to be remembered by the thread of the woman beset by suitors.
We know that the canary and the parsley make a glory
and that the first flute was made from a stolen branch.

We go through ourselves
and having stopped point out the urn and the doves
engraved in the chosen air.
We go through ourselves
and the new surprise gives us our friends
and the birth of a dialectic:
while two dihedrals spin and nibble each other,
the water strolling through the canals of our bones

carries our body toward the calm flow
of the unnavigated land,
where a waking alga tirelessly digests a sleeping bird.
It gives us friends that a light rediscovers
and the square where they converse without being awakened.
From that urn maliciously donated,
there come leaping couples, contrasts and the fever
grafted into the magnet horns
of the crazy page boy making a slick torture even more subtle.
My shame, the magnet horns smeared with a cold moon,
but the scorn gave birth to a cipher
and now unconsciously swung on a branch.
But after offering his respects,
when two-headed people, crafty, correct,
strike with algal hammers the tenor-voiced android,
the chief of the tribe descended the staircase.
The beads they have given us as gifts
have fortified our own poverty,
but since we know we are naked
being will come to rest upon our crossed steps.
And while they were daubing us in wild colors
so we would leap out of the funeral urn,
we knew that as always the wind was rippling the waters
and some steps were following with delight our own poverty.
The steps fled with the first questions of sleep.
But the dog bitten by light and by shadow,
by tail and head;
the dog of dark light that cannot engrave it
and of stinking shadow; the light doesn't refine it
nor does the shadow nurture it: and so it bites

the light and the fruit, the wood and the shadow,
the mansion and the son, breaking the buzz
when the steps go away and he knocks at the portico.
Poor silly river that finds no way out
nor the doors and leaves swelling their music.
It chose, double against single, the cursed clods,
but I don't choose my shoes in a show window.

As it lost its shape on the leaf
the worm sniffed and inspected its old home;
as it bit the waters that had come to the defined river,
the hummingbird touched the old moldings.
The violin of ice shrouded in reminiscence.
The colibri unbraids a music and ties a music.
Our forests don't force man to become lost,
the forest is for us a harmonium in reminiscence.
Every naked man that comes along the river,
in the current or in the glassy egg,
swims in the air if he suspends his breath
and stretches out indefinitely his legs.
The mouth of the flesh of our wood
burns the rippled drops.
The chosen air is like an ax
for the flesh of our wood,
and the hummingbird pierces it.

My back is irritated and furrowed by the caterpillars
that chew some wicker changed into centurion fish,
but I go on working the wood,
like a sleepless fingernail,
like a harmonium that ties and unbraids in reminiscence.

The forest, breathed upon,
releases the hummingbird of the instant
and the old moldings.
Our wood is a toy ox;
the city state is today the state and a small forest.
The guest breathes upon the horse and the rains, too.
The horse rubs its muzzle and its tail over the harmonium of the
    forest;
the naked man intones his own poverty,
the colibri stains and pierces him.
My soul is not in an ashtray.

· JI ·

RHAPSODY FOR THE MULE

Surefootedly, indeed, the mule steps into the abyss.

The mule is slow, and does not sense its mission,
its destiny to toil facing rock, rock that bleeds
to engender the wide-mouthed laughter of pomegranates.
Its hide cracked, the mule is a tiny triumph in the darkness now,
a tiny splotch of mud on sightless wings.
The blindness, glassy stare, and water in your eyes
possess a hidden tendon's strength,
and so those unchanging eyes go surveying
a darkness progressive and ungraspable.
The watery expanse between
the mule's eyes and the gaping tunnel before them
pinpoints its midpoint, girthing it
like the necessary load of lead
that proceeds to fall with the sound
of the mule falling into the abyss.

As salvational wings are nonexistent on a mule,
the girth bolsters its body in the abyss
better than it manages to keep in one place
the load of lead weighing the mule's bowels down

as it falls onto the damp earth
where the trampled rocks have names.
Surefooted and girthed by God,
the mighty mule enters the abyss.

One after another the canyon rings file by
— ring above ring growing larger —
and there on high the carrion
of age-old birds whose necks
display ring after ring.

Continuing its step into the abyss:
the mule is powerless, engenders nothing, declines pursuit,
its eyes do not bulge out
or seek what refuge might be found
along the fertile ledges of the earth.
The mule engenders nothing, which is perhaps like saying:
Does it not feel, not love, not question?
Love beguiled by rose-colored wings,
childlike in its dark conch shell.
The mule feels love for the canyon's
four signs, for the ring after ring
it ascends, glassy-eyed and shortsighted
like a dark body swelled
by primordial waters at the source,
and not redemptive or perfumed ones.
The mule's step is a step into the abyss.

Its gift is sterility no more: it engenders
that surefooted march into the abyss.
The mule is the canyon's friend, its jowls

puff out beneath the lead's tremendous swelling.
Its eyes hold vats of water
and the juice from those eyes
— dirt-stained teardrops —
is its lofty offering for redemption.
The mule's eye grows befuddled in the abyss
and continues in the dark amid its four signs.
Its eyes hold rungs of water,
but facing the sea now
the wave flows back like a body flipping over
at the moment of its sudden death.
The mule is swollen with a valiant swell
that leads it to fall, swollen, into the abyss.
. Settled in the eye of the mule,
glassy and shortsighted, the abyss
slowly scans its own invisibility.
And there in the settled abyss,
step after step, nothing can be heard
but the questions the mule
lets drop upon the rocks over the fire.

Amid the four signs now,
the mule's girthed body settles
upon the coil of calcined rocks.
As it penetrates deeper into the abyss,
its hide trembles as if the rapid questions
bouncing off the canyon walls were nails.
There is only the step of the mule in the abyss.
Its four eyes of wet tinder
wrap rapid glances around the rocks.

Its four feet, the four fettered
signs, revert to rock.
Only a whirl of flying sparks keeps this
from turning into the same old routine.
By now the mule is accustomed — as it is used to its blanket —
to stopping dead in the unbroken darkness,
to falling to the ground, swollen
by nocturnal waters and patient moons.
In the eyes of the mule brim vats of water.
God tightens the girth on the mule
and swells it with lead, as if this were its reward.
While the prancing buck nips at the fire
in the canyon, the mule continues on its way,
advancing like the waters impelled
by the eyes of the fettered.
The mule's step is a step into the abyss.

The sweat flowing down its hooves
soothes the rock pulled off
a fire not schooled in pots,
but in the middle of the skylight, lying darkly.
The mule's step onto the rock is fresh meat
formed from a shining awakening
in the sealed-off, darkening sierra.
The mule is awake now, its magic halter
sealing off the canyon begun
by the buckling of its misty knees.
That surefooted step of the mule into the abyss
is often confused with the prissy gloves of sterility,
confused with the beginnings

of a dark head shaking no in denial.
It is often confused because of you, glassy-eyed outcast,
because of you, lustrous lasso-covered flank,
you who appear to be telling us I do not exist, I do not exist,
but who also set foot in stately homes
where chandeliers no longer provide light
and handheld lamps are moved about
illuminating horror after horror.
It is often confused because of you, glassy outcast,
for the mule's step is a step into the abyss.

The girth of God continues to be of use.
Thus, only when it isn't sparks is the fall
a rock flipping over,
hurling forth meaning like a smooth fire
that leaves untouchable tooth marks behind.
Thus, girth strapped tightly on, as God wills,
the mule's bowels do not revert to its body,
but squeeze out the expression that follows all death.
Overladen body, your leaden bowels
are yet to be discovered in the abyss,
for in taking that terrible plunge
interspersed with dazzling blind spots,
a windmill vane flipping over, unceasingly obscure,
you have placed the two abysses in the shape of a cross.

Your end is not always a plunge into two abysses.
The mule's eyes seem to transport
a moist tree to the bowels of the abyss,
not a tree branching out in green grooves,
but one constricted like the singular voice of beginnings.

Befuddled, as God wills,
the mule continues hauling visible trees
in its eyes and, on the muscles of its back,
the trees that have rejected music.
The shade-giving tree and the figurative tree, too,
have reached the final ring the mule has filed by.
The mule's swollen halter hauls in the tide
while on its neck swim the voices
needed to rise from the void up to the face of the abyss.

A step is a step, and with its vats of water, girthed by God,
the mighty mule trembles in its sleep.
With eyes settled and watery,
in the end the mule slips trees into every abyss.

· GJR ·

JOYFUL NIGHT

The hut by the seashore has kept for one night the naked body of the solitary fisherman. Sleep has been restless, but that unabandoned reality of the lynx-eyed paintbrush accompanies him like a cloak of dew. His turnings on the accompanying quilt were due to the bright stages of moving fire, which even in sleep assured the supreme dignity of movement. When his eyes flashed, his body was already rising from the bed: a good way to answer the ray of light with a movement of the body. Now his body is amid the waves and the sinister lantern of the enemy shore undulates like the whims of the enemy beast. In successive conversations with the sleeping fish his body advances, laughing at its reflections. An arm, a leg, but always the body as a pursued sign ends in a perpetual dignity. How could the body in emerging from sleep and the hut already be prepared for the trembling definition of the current? When he arrives the earth is still silent and nocturnal, but the pilgrim touches it with his forehead and his pursued sign, and in a rhythmical curve his body now prepares to pursue the lantern of the shore left behind. The silence of his body accompanied by the song of the fish, by the curled-up blood of the coral accordions and by the trees of fireflies that come down to the shore to touch the body of the solitary fisherman. And the trees seem to greet both a man and the friendly fragrance of the dye bark. He has penetrated again the hut on the shore, but now he has found it all illuminated. His body trans-fused in a light sent from elsewhere seems to show forth in a Participation, and the Lord, just and benevolent, smiles an exquisite smile. But the fisherman does not interrupt his joy in the Presence, spurts out a curved stream of water, reminiscence of love for the enemy shore and the benevolent hut, and says to us, *What has passed through here?*

FABULOUS CENSURES

Quickly, the water is reabsorbed nervously into the corpuscle; slow it is, like the invisible splashing of lead. The crevices, the dry protuberances are pulled to the same level by the whalelike passage of the water. It covers Tartaruses, Barathrums, and Depths, and does not sleep in its extension because of the hum. Who hears? Who pursues? The very rock, previously a freezing, cooks in the straight decisive swift corpuscle sent by the light the new bodies of the dance. The receptacle creaks sluggishly, and the shark — slow breadth of silver in the accelerated breadth of lead — gradually shows his smile, his leisurely and total frenzy. A shred of veined copper stays over his tail, a laughing dolphin hovers on the dorsal fin. The slow column of impelled horizontal lead has fulfilled its role of closing off the deformities and nobilities, the gentle silver and the corrugated iron. The smoke of secreted evaporation has gesticulated in the rocky casserole, which thus afflicts the stone with the very brief touch of a thread torn loose from Energy. The shark that has been able to breathe in the column of lead, matching the stream he has breathed with the color of his skin, in all later years has continued in the water with the muscular jubilance of a star outside the window. The breeze was a guide: testimony of each pore used by the opal, the scorpion, and the hoopoe. The body of the shark forced the chorus of rocks surrounding his neck, while the light like an oxyhydrogen torch painted animals and flowers on his venerable face. Applying himself then to the innermost part of the rocks, he provoked the dynasty and destiny of the roots spreading out in galleries where the perverse flow of lunar liquid had circulated. The rock is the Father, the light is the Son. The breeze is the Holy Spirit.

THE ADHERING SUBSTANCE

If we left our arms in the ocean for two years the toughness of our skin would be strengthened until it bordered on the greatest and noblest of animals and on the monster that comes at the call of soup and bread. Crude latherings with the tegument of a horse. Chew a crab and breathe it out through our fingertips while playing the piano. Qualities that come and are repulsed with slowness, with displeasure and propriety. With celestial disgust. With celestial scorn for frivolity and the errant, wayward stamp, the submerged arm dignifies its cramps and its absent whiteness; it endures the sleep of the tides first, and the miserable jewels that drill through its flesh until they are blessed by a rosy doubling dew, perhaps to make with them a region of sands like eyes, where the hollow pincer, the shameful foot are transported with the natural swiftness of air thickened by hard and silver light. The submerged arm, as it is turned into a lodging for centerings and bubbles, intractable hump for resolute informers, finds itself circled by the insect like a flying point; while the snail like an insistent point, frantic yet very very slow, becomes encrusted on that portion, flesh and earth, pounded with masterly craft by the renewed numbers of the waves. Thus that submerged fragment, secured by the trial period of peace, is returned by echo and reflux as a superhuman, very very white mystery. As the years go by, the submerged arm does not become a marine tree; on the contrary it returns a larger statue, with an improbable yet palpable body, a similar body for that submerged arm. Very very slow, as from life to sleep; as from sleep to life, very very white.

FIFES, EPIPHANY, GOATS

Clarities became dark. Until then darkness had been a diabolic sloth, and clarity a contented insufficiency of the creature. Unchanged dogmas, clear darknesses, which the blood in spurts and in continuity resolved, like the butterfly caressing the shepherd's forehead while he sleeps. A birth that was before and after, before and after the abysses, as if the birth of the Virgin were prior to the appearance of the abysses. *Nondum eram abyssi et ego jam concepta eram.* The delectable mystery of the sources that will never be resolved. The rejected uncooked clay now cooked, already leaping outside origins for grace and wisdom. The Book of Life that begins with a metaphor and ends with the vision of Glory is all filled with You. And Yours is the tremendous punishment, the sudden decapitation: You can erase from the Book of Life. Eternal Life, which arches from man clarified by Grace to the nocturnal tree, can declare mortal, strike down, release the spark. Once the erasure is made, a new name comprising a new man occupies its place, which thus does not even leave behind the shadow of its hollowness, the scandal of its ashes. Tremendous drought now erased by the goats of familiar contentment, by the pipes of overturnings and colors. Herd together, stumble, understand yourselves, more deeply if one is disposed to be born, to march toward the youthfulness that is becoming eternal. Until the arrival of Christ, Pascal said, only *false peace* had existed; after Christ, we may add, true warfare has existed. The warfare of partisans, of witnesses killed in battle, the hundred and forty and four thousand, offered as first fruits unto God and to the Lamb (Revelation, 14:3 and 4): And they sung as it were a new song before the throne. Herd together, stumble, goats; begin at last, pipes, God and man are now alone. Tremendous drought, blaze of sun: I go toward my forgiveness.

WEIGHT OF FLAVOR

Seated within my mouth I attend the landscape. The great white tuba establishes nonspiraloid mumblings, bridges, and linkages. In that tuba, the paper and the large drop of lead fall slowly but without causality. Although if we withdraw the mat of our tongue and suddenly confront the palatine vault, the paper and the drop of lead could not stand the terror. Then, the paper and the drop of lead downward are like the tortoise upward but without ascending. If we were to withdraw the mat. . . . Thus the flavor that tends to stand out, if we were to tear out its tongue, would multiply in perennial arrivals, as if our door were continually attended by bulldogs, Chinese beggars, angels (the order of angels called Thrones, that rapidly place things in God), and long-tailed crustaceans. When the mat is sliced, turning the emptiness into an inquisitive though eyeless fish, the vocal cords receive the flow of dark dampness, beginning the monody. A dark lurch and the echo of the vocal cords, the night thus pursuing the night, the waning cat's back pursuing the dragonfly, obtaining the necessary amount of whiteness so that the messenger can go through the wall. The sheet of paper and the drop of lead go toward the luminous circle of the abdomen that extends its fires to receive the visitor and keep away the speckled agony of the pitiful tiger. The weightiness of the palatine vault grinds up even the breath, deciding that the luminous ray must advance amid the colloidal states formed by the revolutions of the solids and the liquids in their first inaugural fascination, when the beginnings revolve, as yet unable to detach the ages. Later, the successions will always maintain a nostalgia for the limited single specimen, the white peacock or the buffalo that hates mud, but with nearness forever attained and accessible, as if we could only walk on the mat. Seated within my mouth I notice death moving like the motionless fir submerging its icy glove in the trash of the pond. An inverse custom had made for me the opposite marvel, in dreams during afternoon naps I thought it a consummate obligation — seated now in my mouth I contemplate the darkness surrounding the fir — for the scribe to wake up day after day as a palm tree.

DEATH OF TIME

In a vacuum velocity dares not compare itself, can caress the infinite. Thus the vacuum is defined and inert as a world of nonresistance. Also the vacuum sends out its first negative graph so it can be like nonair. The air we were accustomed to feel (to see?): soft as a sheet of glass, hard as a wall or a sheet of steel. We know by an almost invisible stirring of the nonexistence of an absolute vacuum that there cannot be an infinite unconnected to divisible substance. Thanks to that we can live and are perhaps fortunate. But let us suppose some implausibilities in order to gain some delights. Let us suppose the army, the silk cord, the express train, the bridge, the rails, the air that constitutes itself as another face as soon as we draw close to the window. Gravity is not the tortoise kissing the ground. The express train always has to be stopped on a bridge with a broad rock base. It impels itself — like the impulsion of his smile to laughter, to raucous laughter, in a feudal lord after his garnished dinner — , until it decapitates tenderly, until it dispenses with the rails, and by an excess of its own impulsion slips along the silk cord. That velocity of infinite progression tolerated by a silk cord of infinite resistance comes to feed upon its tangencies that touch the ground with one foot, or the small box of compressed air between its feet and the back of the ground (lightness, angelisms, nougat, larks). The army in repose has to rest upon a bridge with a broad rock base, impels itself and comes to fit, in hiding, behind a small poplar, then in a worm with a backbone grooved by an electric time. The velocity of progression reduces the tangencies, if we suppose it to be infinite, the tangency is pulverized: the reality of the steel box on the archetypal rail, in other words the silk cord, is suddenly stopped, the constant progression derives another independent surprise from that temporal tangency, the air turns as hard as steel, and the express train cannot advance because the potency and the resistance become infinite. There is no fall because of the very intensity of the fall. While potency turns into ceaseless impulsion, the air mineralizes and the moving box — successive, impelled —, the silk cord and the air like steel refuse to be replaced by the crane on one foot. Better than substitution, restitution. To whom?

PROCESSION

The parade of the numbers took place in the tedium of its invincible fall, a malaise tolerated as proof of its comfortable succession. Within the numbers there were successions and meanings: if the successions motivated their friendly groupings, the meanings motivated the challenging fluidity of their rhythms. The parades of the binary of war, the elusive sequence of the fish, forgot their origins and their ends, their impulsion and their extenuated frenzy, in order to give us in the muscles of the leopard the finest geometrical progressions, in navigating magnets a ridiculous and unforgettable limitation. The fascinations of those archetypal groupings, of the magnetizing that convokes in order to flee from the whirl that must be reduced to the law of its structure, gradually brought about the end of the cynic, the atomist and the pre-Augustinian Alexandrine. *The vendor of words.* Man propagates and injures his substance, God superabounds, the encounter takes place in His generosities. But the beginning, at false and visible moments, seemed to be separated from the Other. From then on, men will form two groups: those who believe that the generosity of the One engenders sameness, and those who believe that it leads it to Darkness, to the Other. Thus the procession which in emerging from Form is prolonged until it passes through and is submerged by ultimate Essence, is saved yet again by being filled with the symbolic and concupiscible figure that encloses the already illuminated substance. And thus where the Stoic thought that he leapt out of his skin into a void, the Catholic situates the procession in order to awake in his body as a limit, the adventure of the same real and richly possible substance in order to awake in Him. When he dies, the Procession has become so inordinate that the plasticity of the chorale is replaced by an echo that seems to turn back again toward us, already extending hands, walking another cross. In the snow, in the defile, in the chosen mansion, the procession of men goes on dividing by similarity, occupying, betraying, or communicating the same body, the blood and the oils.

TANGENCIES

After inventing the zero, Prince Aleph-Zero proceeded on horseback until sleep was put across his path, throwing him from his horse toward the grass that covered soft spongiform rocks. The horse's arrow is his nose. He placed his knife between the ground and himself, and then placed his shield over the knife with malicious inclination, since through there his sleep was going to pass. As the knife moved over the ground, the fountain gushed forth, but the seed was dying. In the first disasters of sleep, he had leaned with his somnolent bow on the vertical thrust of the recent fountain, in such a way that the bow resting on what he could glimpse was hardened horizontally; increasing its potency the jet of the fountain touched both the man detached from the air and his sleep so lightly that he could keep himself horizontal without giving up the sleep that had detached him from his horse. Sleep amputated him from his horse, making him feel that as he abandoned it he abandoned himself, so that then he could regain the impenetrable hardness of the same sleep crossed upon the clock within the fountain. Again the horse throws its hyaline crewman through sleep. The horse that savors arsenic rejects tortoise shell powder. The cargo thrown by the horse into the fountain keeps his forehead softly resting on the edge of the window. He is not the inventor of the zero, he is the inventor of the sling and seed, the one who waits until the water rots so that the planetary memory of the seed may begin. The marvelous man, on the contrary, at the corner of his garden of triangular and lozenge-shaped flagstones, squats on his legs and stretches out his arms like a swan fed with diorite cotton. Even at night, a tribune gymnast, losing his memory, a retrospective acidity with a patina, hemmed in by his rhythmic, copious, trembling scratches. At midnight, the man of the seed with his face cut drops his head softly on the edge of the window, which also supports the two feet of the man in the green, orange, and gray tights of steel mesh, taking the corner of his garden like a rope in a port. Each separated by the edge of the window, the man of earth arches his eye more to listen than to discover, while the gymnast, in the same midnight of startled normality, raises and lowers his legs in a rhythm that seems like the memory of a march along the river. When he deposited the seed, he could not know that it was pierced through, support for a night when thrown from the horse. The gymnast, abruptly shifting the tiny rubber ball with a steel center from his hand of remembered smoke to his other hand of bitten gold, opens his eyes and linearity in his weariness, exhausting himself to attain the height, duration, and weight of a saurian. It is not strange that whenever he finally throws the instruments with which he strengthened the steadiness of his hands, he should stumble upon a flower because of his fatigue, and that each monstrous fatigue should be paralyzed with the earthborn attached burning sensation of the seed pierced through by the man thrown from the horse.

ECSTASY OF THE
DESTROYED SUBSTANCE

And you, Promachus, close the double chain of ants. Did you count the cattle? Destroy the body and the sign of its hollowness so as to attain the reminiscence of its transparency. Destroy the inverse relationship of unity and substance, of number and perceptible thing, resolved in the figure detached by the ecstasy of participation in the homogeneous. But first, the sphere is encompassed by the boy's hand. The violent substitution followed by a hollow gust prepares the void, the whale, and the bottle, where there is coming and going as by a principal originator, covered with smoke and extremely hurried. Now, blind am I. I encompass and understand myself, blackened in the bottle that contains the dead armillary sphere suspended by boreal magnets. Blind am I, my home is the whale. Alongside the void, I emit my yawn or give away plaster hats, and an immense funerary ceramic takes from the temple those who have been decapitated in order to establish with their simultaneous fury a dense hum of memories. Thus, in a marshy grotto, with a waltzed floor squeezed from tortoise eggs, the master watchmaker trembles at the frightful coincidences and the fleur-de-lys–covered farmer receives, as he sows the only false document, the shameless blessings of the law. The substitution of metaphor and act, pulverizing the thing in itself, illuminating it like a stained-glass window distributing the light of day. The ecstasy of what is beautiful in itself breathes a participating breath into the thing in itself, because of the transparency of man and the reading of the rocks. Linear development of instant, erotics, being (unity), existing (act), metaphor (substitution of being), participation (substitution of existing), Paradise (ecstasy of participation in the homogeneous, intemporality). Linearity broken or swollen by the three circular moments of germ, entity, eternity, necessary for taking over their refuge, leaving at the door Doctor Faust's flaming dog. The destruction of substance, illuminating its variants or metamorphoses, because of the dryness of its suspension or withdrawals. The Son of Man destroyed, transformed into the lasting substance of the body of God, because all transfigurations are followed by a suspension and the exercise on the Mount of Skulls was only an apprenticeship for being plunged into a violent and superhuman negative capacity. Frantic self-destruction which makes all metamorphosis ridiculous, in order to reach the constant germ within the entity. The power of the scorpion — Revelation 9:5 — which does not attack any green thing but instead attacks only the men who have no seal on their foreheads. The power of the scorpion in alliance with the *splendor formae*. Natural substance does not change. The rational soul receives the intelligible light by means of the illuminated figure or plenitude. When the witness exclaims: *only thus does a god die,* he has been broken and has fallen in battle against the mute or incessant waking spirit.

RESISTANCE

Resistance always has to destroy the act and the potency which demand the antithesis of the corresponding dimension. In the world of *poiesis,* opposed in so many things to the world of physics, which is the world we have had since the Renaissance, resistance has to proceed by rapid inundations, by total trials that do not want to adjust, clean, or define the crystal, but rather to surround, to open a breach through which water may fall tangent to the turning wheel. Potency is, like hail, everywhere, but resistance recovers itself in the danger of not being in the earth or in hail. The demon of resistance is nowhere, and therefore it presses like the mortar and the broth, and keeps leaving its mark like the fire in the golden glitter of visions. Resistance assures that all the wheels are turning, that the eye sees us, that potency is a delegated power dropped upon us, that it is the nonself, things, coinciding with the darkest self, with the stones left in our waters. Hence the eyes of potency do not count, and in resistance what crosses our path, springing either from ourselves or from a mirror, is reorganized into eyes with currents passing through them that perhaps may never belong to us at all. Compared with resistance, morphology is completely ridiculous. What morphology allows, the realization of an epoch in a style, is very scant in comparison to the eternal resistance of what is not permissible. Potency is merely the permission granted.

Method: not even intuition, not even what Duns Scotus called con-
fused abstract knowledge, reason in disarray. Method: not even cre-
ative vision, since total resistance prevents the organizations of the
subject. When resistance has overcome the quantitative, the ancestral
recollections of the steward and the last sterile figurations of the qual-
itative, then the man they have repented making begins to boil, the
man made and set loose, but with a daily repentance for having made
him by the one who made him. Then. . . . *On this night, at the begin-
ning of it, they saw fall from the sky a marvelous branch of fire into the sea,
at a distance from them of four or five leagues* (Journal of Voyage, 15
September 1492). Let us not fall into the idea of paradise regained, for
the men who came packed into a ship moving within a resistance
could see a branch of fire fall into the sea because they felt the history
of many in a single vision. Those are the times of salvation and their
sign is a fiery resistance.

• JI •

TO REACH MONTEGO BAY

(Permission to feel a slight shock.)

Furiously I abjure you and classically
summon you I, a grim restless laurel, down
to this same low ring of cold, to the harvest
of altar tablets for sowing and for art.

From that glass bathed in the waters of its orphanhood
more may be had, sun-baked souls at Advent, than from trusting
in the cord-thick rain or the wind's great remove
when its gusts strike your sides in search of their pith.

They say that badgers, in the waters of their wetness,
do engrave more, their snouts pointy tips for cutting through
the shadow of a skirmish in a jug of wine,
replaced by the maid of the fat millennium.

For if the gust did blow that way —
the one passing its hat between the two cymbals —
now a foolish maneuver takes the heater by surprise
and in comes the butler, rubbing his hands, before withdrawing
    again.

The laburnum brought to mind the plains of Plataea
while the amaranth mocked the grapes in the grapefruit grove
as the fruit-vendor, like Parthenopes in search of a breeze,
takes off his shoes, leaps the moon, and makes the head steward's
    beard grow.

There is dignity in the coin with the head of the Corinthian girl,
in the rustics looking for bugs in their accordions
as the coal that is woven knocks against the ship's side
and the cliff bellows in the grimy lady's clothes closet.

The maiden is the popess, the snail, and the mayor,
the stiff drinks of the tax collector from the west;
my decoded yell shatters the maiden's hatchet
and, better yet, the grapefruit grove and new season of stalactites.

She is no foot darning pillars held by the heel
or mailman's bag, a calendar of saints with incredible births,
not a pigeon tracing the initials of filigreed citizenry
or a bumblebee painting the old biddy's bee.

As woodsmen do not carry hatchets to swear an oath
and the captain does not talk in his sleep, flicking his fingers,
so do lines of verse, sugar-coated and devoted at stud,
announce the rain, the trogon bird, the trespass, the close friend.

It must be the old biddy's bee, Hermes affirms,
as it cannot be the bee's old biddy, affirms Euphorion.
The bee alights between the slouch hat and the honey,
between sweet foolishness and the dry, funereal kind.

The canon in the mortar sullies your nose, the gold
part presenting itself as the stew from some Bavarian
toyland. The eye has no reason to look like the sun.
Oh, Gulfweed Jehovah, blast that bragging with a comet!

After the mason wounds the tapir on its yellow forehead,
he is struck by a bullet that turns him into a doe from *Río
Grande do Sul.* The year's charming gesture has artifice
jumbling together the Chief's moons, necklaces, and chamois
    jackets.

There is no reason to carry firebrands at the abduction.
Days before witnessed the catty measurements of windows,
and two days before, half-moons, the cold horseshoes
given us by Furgan, the English coal miner's son.

He reappeared in town with his charm and his dream,
his charm the highlight of the dream
and his dream the fortress of a charm heightened
by stars that sleep and beaches that stay awake.

To reach *Montego Bay,*
sullen adolescent fury concealed its arrows,
not its withdrawal from participation in absence,
settling, instead, into the digging and the hole.
Aversion exists to playing the wax tablet, to hiding the king of
    spades
in a handkerchief, to hearing the *obbligato* marmoreal
cymbal clash of belly laughs launched in the attack
and not perforation with the zenith's stick pin, but the cloaked

act of covering the plum tree with that other lunar flesh
when off we go demanding the almond tree's bone
and the branches that show us the alleluia of the blossom
if not the honey flowing down the secret of the pistils,
crystallizing into sodden lumps for our pleasure in the blue-
    mountain
bower, lumps that trip the traveler up
and, in a one-two-three, crack him half open
among the mocking laughter or in the seven rivers drawn
by a team of oxen.

The pools where the coral heirs take a dip —
British heirs who have smiled amid Egyptian excavations —
furrow out ripples, dissecting them from capitalist decadence.
One undergoes as many trials in a cigarette ad
as at the start of a Minoan funeral.
The abbreviated images in Syracusan mirrors, cut off
by the shutter of a squirrel's tail,
enlarge their venerable toucan eyelids
to reach *Montego Bay.*

The huge black preacher taking nodding coins from a Mozartean
    waistcoat —
a porter's lodge of marsupial pockets the waistcoat was, too —
opened his flaccid arms like a centurion in the pool
before needing the smelling salt's bracing synthesis to flex them
    again.
The thickset bats of the Jamaican bay,
ridding themselves of all reflections off the myrtle pool,
penetrated the cuneiform markings on the inside of a palm tree's
    trunk.

A mammee-apple railroad flowed from the black giant's mouth,
his weepy flesh rocked gently by the sweet guitar of nerves
as he left us the guise of a real scare
in the pool at *Montego Bay.*

As happens with the open cartridge belts of drunken soldiers,
the black preacher made the loosened half of his waistcoat pale
before the pool rippled by the triple jump of the Greeks' Heraclean
    stone.
His waistcoat, like a hardened moss bodice,
displayed his funny androgynous flirting in *Montego Bay,*
not in the infernal bower where bats penetrate tree trunks,
but in the charge of the leafy autumn clouds expelled
by the *fire of the florest.* The refinement of the coconut
grove matches the orange fringe of the Austrian cockatoo,
for a slimness that once seemed unsurpassable is now everywhere to
    be found
like Achaean ships burning before the frivolity of Ilion.
The refinement of the coconut grove tosses chewed-up,
spit-covered seeds onto the stylization of ads
for cigarette brands in *Montego Bay.*

The lawn's obsequious carnality has spent itself
waiting for a twilight of musical interludes.
That *flamboyant,* the royal poinciana, like Miss Albino Giraffe,
stretched its stiff trunk toward the flute's candied crystal
while a Tunisian hat's small red crown
towered with its tapered flame atop the inquisitive black man
tamely entangled in his disguise as a mailman in *Her Majesty's*
    service.

A pack of young burros and a decorated Rolls
stretched out before the sergeant directing traffic with an admiral's
    binoculars.
But as happens with the priestly elements of Ionic physics,
the *fire of the florest* was replaced by *laughing falls*
and the belly laughs of the seven confluent waters,
effacing the useless stickpin from the straitjacketed fire
before reaching *Montego Bay.*

The coconut grove and the unshaded tapering
of the *fuego de la floresta* make sprigs of the sesquipedalian sway:
the long fish is governed by the laws of magnetism.
Palm trees walked about in far-away Eros, for the distance
aroused the irritated skin of remoteness, as between us each palm
casts forth the voluptuous counterpoint of its ambit; and thus a
    glance
recognizes its own carnality in the palpus on the cuirass of the night.
The coconut grove compels vegetative growth
by pursuing a spark or the star fallen into the rancher's
sack of coal. That *flamboyant,* the royal poinciana, must raise
the Bengal studs on its crown so that the circle of coconut trees
does not chip the unexpected coral off this vaguely glimpsed
    studding.
The copulating bay where the heavyset arrive with marrow
from the kneecaps of young black goats, invades the coconut grove
with the torpor of its shade, squeezing the very waist of its pith.
That tapering in pursuit of the leaping spark
may only be penetrated through the shady broth of its wide bottom.
The lamination creaks and rots from the thickening evaporation
of the waters; if it did not, its angelic transparency would equal in
    meaning

the vertical thickness of vegetable meat, and the latest swimmer
would be motionless between this penetrability of thickness and
    angelic
transparency; if not, the waters' evaporated shade might penetrate
    still
the coconut groves of *Montego Bay*.

The seven rivers meet in a belly laugh, and the symmetry
of the wooded grove is fashioned for the subtlety of the moribund
    insect,
for there a man feels the scenery scolding
a belly laugh poised on his shoulders, lulling him to sleep.
The seventeen salads on the *Hotel de los Mirtos* menu
were created with the flying-antelope carpet in mind, not for the
    heavy sleep
of the lad in the eclogues or the devices of his sizable flute.
The surging waves of vegetation passed unacknowledged by the
    swimmer
who made do with a mound where vegetative evaporations
failed to recall the ashes used in the portentous wind's solemnities.
Her Majesty's mail service takes solace in forgetting addresses,
for the postal customer has nodded off in this endless vegetable
    destiny,
his whistle failing to penetrate the funeral pyramid's drowsing shell.
The scenery — for the insect's genitalia and not man's memory —
is what sets spinning the loony moons of the surging waves
in *Montego Bay*.

The laminated, much-pursued waists of coconut groves,
nibbled by the shady marrow awakened in the bay,
hurled forth the spark that colors the distance for the insect's

Eros and its labyrinthine lot of pollen and sand.
Erotic remoteness denotes the swaying extension of the starry sky,
but once the spark fell in the bay when the heavyset and blind
arrived, they did not unclasp their hands at the birth of the singing
    fish
in *Montego Bay*.

The dry tongue showed prominent disfigurations
after the valley and the first bay moved
into the submerged garden, a damp bluish dust
coating the marmoreal tortoise and stalactic lotus both.

Medieval paintings of leaves, mocking nature's dew,
dotted like freckles the book of parallel, sunken hours.
Once these leaves brandished virescent banderillas,
their flesh was preserved like the dusty bodies of dynasties.

The tail, the tongue, the humble little arm, too, all smiled friskily
in the anthologized experience of submerged design
or overextended clarity, which disappears when folding
into spoony eye-locks or tourniquets of penetrating fury.

Attending to a leaf is well worth the homage of containing
fire within strict boundaries, well worth suckling
dolphins frolicking amid the shining seaweed,
raising smoky consecrations on their pontifical spines.

Properties and appurtenances compelled me to furrow
my rusted blood as the countryside went pinning
another insect to the felt with its moon, for its swift lamination
was not made for the staff taking root in the snow.

It arrived with the blood when it breaks both circles,
the big one and small one inexhaustible and furious, but the
    garrulous
mystery of our blood returned after much hurry,
after it penetrated someone else's bay and both arms of the sea.

When questioned, the sea froth spits its salt factories forth.
If we penetrate the council of the tide from behind,
the blood's rancor will flow back through both hatches,
for the nondual mystery welcomes and blinds what enmity is
    allowed.

The sea does not rush off to the seizing of the cask,
for spermatic blood disentangled itself in another body,
abandoning the useless mystery tugging on the trees
and the questions, like caterpillars, a walled-in labyrinth of leaves.

What once was abduction now grows accustomed to siestas in the
    sand;
the fish lie back literate, the drowsing instruments devoured.
The music-filled mangrove swamp, protecting wide wombs,
also protected the shade that penetrates bodies absent a male.

In *Montego Bay,* the detestable crush of shoulders
about to spread out in a tree where the fresh lad was lowered
brought with it the horror of that first genius who deemed man
and tree equal, thus preserving the breed in a flinty tedium.

The mysterious tribe, predating the first written testimonies,
turned back to the Scythians' amputating horses
but not to the lightning, that abductor of Etruscan kings.

Affectionate taming and piercing the tree's shade proved enough for
   them.

This was the language of the tribe that had escaped writing,
where moving shadow was the fixed shade of the tree.
The sole of the foot put down tiny nocturnal roots
while the palm of the hand hid the breathing, decoded stars.

Scythian tamers savored the dew's divinity
while fearful Nyctimene embodied the damnations of Lesbos.
Voluptuous country estates, awakened by the plantain leaf's
refinement, left the horsemen dew from phallic dreams.

Afterward on the sands, silken pauses interspersed
between the submerged unreal and the dense, irresistible apparition,
the metric aquarium was built and the earth-bound umbilicus
overcame the dissolute horizon confusing man with the
   reproduction of trees.

The temptation in the wilderness was filled with countless white
   oxen
chatting with those who had extracted the mystery of the waters;
the earth, evaporated by the *verbum*'s solitary conjugation,
turns crazed and titanic between the big circle and the small.

The snout would bury itself up to the failure of the well
as bodies groped for the key to two clocks,
but the sunburnt sand does not rise to the gossip
necessary for the vegetation's bowels or the spilled secret.

The principal hills, talking oxen, fell upon the laughter of the bay,
leaping over huts where illegitimate ceramics are made.

With pottery's tradition undone by the futile fish of a Picasso
    Mediterranean,
the devil's sensual, big-nosed ginger slobbered on the fledgling
    trogon bird.

But the man with musical numbers in his ears who went off to wash
    the rings,
freeing himself from both Saturn and the lightness of his skirt-
    chasing meals
by ceremoniously unfurling the bells of the quartet,
would always graciously take his wife along in an overnight bag.

The man from Seville, a castle obstructed by cottony fits of
    trembling,
would welcome us in and, with the pair of us cornered by a
    sugarcane cutter,
start in with his tumultuous caressing and erudite scandals,
yielding himself up with the courtly fears of the dominant male.

The abductor, emerging after restless sleep from the coal mine's
    bowels
in disdain of the Devil Child closing the tall gate,
would catch up with the stray little thing's joyous sunflower,
penetrating through the once-hostile, mid-range voice into the
    breath of Amphion.

· G J R ·

THE MUSIC CAR

In remembrance of Raimundo Valenzuela
and his carnival orchestras.

It is not the car with the covered fire, but the sound is there.
Valenzuela has scattered twelve orchestras through the *Parque*
Central, a crush of Phrygian lamps, affectionate blue-
flannel kiosks and fickle Compostelan tears.

They leap from their siestas and pat down their waistlines
to fly with the flute's Havana impulsions.
The flute is the string pursuing the waistline in sleep.
The waistline is the flute uncovered by wasps.

Like a general that lowers his booming voice to hand out cigarettes
at sentry posts, Valenzuela surveyed the zodiac signs.
Each star showed his orchestra at some casino
table, which Valenzuela kept stocked with sugar.

Sugar with meticulous blood, grapefruit heaped with cinnamon,
with lapis-lazuli sugar. Prophecy in a treacherous soup bowl.
The frock coat on so youthful a figure had no need for taffeta;

he gave no notice before leaping from his car, lounging in squads
   of music.

He would stop to chat with the pipers, with the ironers of ashes,
disdainfully producing the secret key and the offers.
They'd show him the pattern for a pair of pleated trousers
and, with the cloth in his ear, he'd recognize whose unfinished hand
   it came from.

"Carita de rana," "El Gobernador," "Segismundo el vaquero,"
they'd break into a little dance with their goatlike asses
and tangled key rings chewed by the dogs.
A flame, a gunshot, and a shawl cast moonlight on the nets there.

All around the *Parque Central,* Valenzuela's
twelve orchestras played. Four beneath four different trees.
Another four in the dance hall of Compostelan tears.
Three on windy corners. One at One San Rafael.

Have I mentioned the stifling heat, the sun's ember illuminating the
   reed beds,
the aril-rich *mamoncillo* tree on a twisting, half-dry riverbed,
the youthful figure sporting those depressing taffeta bands?
He'd wake up and leap to another orchestra as if on a trapeze.

Between his daybreak and sleep, the orchestra moved like a *majá*
   snake.
Everything he says is written in a column of sound,
the column each man takes fishing with him to the river.
Oh, essence with lightning bolts dotted with dew, in Arab script,
   too!

When an orchestra grows quiet, a figure shows up in relief.
He selects the key for another pyramid of sound
while on high a banana tree looms, a pheasant flutters. A star
adorns the corner of a handkerchief, a gift from White's beloved.

"El dragón," "El bombín," the overheated tiles shout
and, like a mortar, scrape the pine wax off the floor.
The cornet sets the bees from Peru galloping,
but they melt when touched by the oboe's rounded tip.

The party-boy terror, a sweet fifteen, drew back the sheets,
sweating out that frothing she-wolf of an incessant eighth-note
like when chasing a seagull along an embankment on the beach.
As he emerged from sleep, a soft-coal whistle would rock him on
    the seas.

The spinning that sweetens him also makes him wet;
it is still incongruous for him to take his column to the river.
He looks at his haunches and confuses them with a horse's.
A frog's leg interrogates him as if he were the vegetable king.

They take him by the hand to lead him to the orchestral whirlwind,
but he weeps. The whirlwind is a kettledrum where the boy tugs
on the plutonic salamander's tail, then covers
its eyes with stones from the river, stones marked with holes.

Watch, watch, a stubbed toe trips him there;
touch, touch, a carnival soaks him with water.
He grunts as from a knock on the head in the bloodied mirror;
when he's about to strike, a strident laugh handcuffs him with its
    ringlets.

Like a flame driven about in a car,
Valenzuela restores the wet numbers.
A winged mask transports him now to the Compostelan tears
and, with a rhythm darkly imposed upon him, plucks stones from
    his blood.

He goes about uncovering eyes that have grown sleepy for him,
skin sweating to break the roughness of the lizard
viewing among the stones a century fallen from the planet.
This lizard sets aside the stones trampled by a horse with tetanus.

The car with the flame made the marble pillow bright
and then the hand that moved it from the eddy to the cloud.
He emerged from sleep at the eddy, from the eddy at the river
where the king's otter washed the Egyptian diapers.

Wet numbers are not an allusion to the Pythagorean "odd,"
but they did run to a doorway once the drenched woman arrived.
Her trampling on the mask meant the end of the river.
She sat bleeding and naked on a circus horse.

He lent the horse a crook of corn and burr
but it pushed him away with its hoofs the way a broken
bandurria signals the start of a clown's Sunday,
green and black, ceramic china whose tale the tightrope walker tells.

Here, the man needed no music training before he died;
shades did not have to give rhythm advice as they descended into
    hell.
The seed already carried the breeze's measurements
and the shades fled; the number was related by the light.

The early morning hours made the taffeta on Valenzuela's frock
   coat shine.
Now the couple sat in the car handing out Pythagorean warnings
as the flame, inside the car as well, swam upon sleep's undulations
under the sway of the Havana flute's courtly tricorn hat.

The couple reigned in the naturalizing supernatural,
surged forth from sleep and remaining in the Orplid of recognition.
Cigarette butts, dead leaves, gobs of spit, and down quilts are all
   their fortune.
If they dipped a finger in it, the drenched woman's womb would
   swell.

After four seasons, they could no longer meet the eddy's test.
The dance hall became a part of the supernatural one can derive.
To dance is to find the unity formed by the living and the dead.
Whoever dances most plays chess with the blond Rhadamanthus.

The constellation of pipers sits upon the starry bear's back,
but the Havana flute was cutting the taffeta bows short.
It is the same car, though, with a noble mulatto inside.
He waves a long time, in the conflagration, at the melting cornice.

· GJR ·

A VISIT FROM
BALTASAR GRACIÁN

The one who yearns to roam about
is under watch around the clock;
the eel would like to slither out
when it hears whistling through the lock.
Still in one piece, it curls and tucks,
no one can see it, so it plucks
a bracelet — intellect of sand.
By Nature bid that stealth be borne
upon hyena hides as planned,
why should hyenas feel our scorn?

That letter from the devil's pen
burst into flames unread, though hot,
thus Pablo (so-called) scaped again,
sly scamp, retriever, chamber pot.
The souls who fell prey to this sham
were disappointed at their ease.
They never found within the breeze
what arches on the feline's back.

No inkwell and no paper lined,
a phantom of the printer's mind.

At midnight on his jailhouse skip,
St. John knocks at the convent's gate:
Please let me in, I've broken free.
Feast of the pomegranate tree.
Gracián then gives his coach the slip,
a wit but for the accent's weight.
Thus gravitas on shadow's wing,
the shadow and the printer, too,
draw ash out of the inkwell's slue
and roll it out like carpeting.

Good Glaucon, froth his watermark,
a god who has the eel well read,
makes it immortal, spinning thread
not in the sea, but in the dark,
avoiding counterpoint and stitch.
The eel's immortalizing pitch
crowns Cronion, the beetle-browed,
not in fresh waters, but in brine,
and slipping in his huge mouth's shroud-
ing, falls for good from man's sight line.

If keen to flee his order's oath,
entangled in sure friendship's doubt,
with Lastanosa he'd sweat out
his nephew and disorder both
in epigram and sonnet form.
He's somberness perfected, born

of thread his shadow long has cast.
He hatches plots, which no one spies,
a shadow who gives names that last
to night and even oxen eyes.

These very ornaments, the issue of an obsidian
sword, breathe like a hide that is drummed upon.
They asked questions with Aldebaran's bagpipes, the starry
chill of an escutcheon at the inn on their journey home.
Fish are there, leather shields, curses, and falling bodies
that enter riddled like the corn, incompatible,
while their ant-hoarded gold, fractions of melodious tiaras,
sticks out like a tower in a mass of equestrian blue.
A slight start, and that tireless child combatant,
a coppery hallucinated mist, runs off to a game of *brisca*
inside the castle where a bishop's miter rests on every chair.

"How much for a jug of wheat?" he asks
above the barking that surrounds a solemn promise.
"Approach within earshot of the throne and lean over the
    marble-colored
horn striking the ear of the buck's spitting image."
Again he turns toward the tapestry, though his gaze directs him to
    the dogs.
Again he turns toward the tapestry, for midnight's smoky haze
will not always present you with the gift of flight.
His hands choke the artificial buck, helping
unravel the loose thread cutting off
its ears to isolate it from embossment in the wind.

· GJR ·

SURPRISED

I can't. I mean it. And the horse begins bending the poker deck.
Just a minute. The grapefruit's cleared of rain. I'm spelling.
What question fits? What elbow intermingles?
The thurifer has soaked himself, withdrawing.
These are witnesses, oaths, platitudes.
An index finger crooked as a nose,
pointless, cinders, rounding off.
A cardboard riposte. Certain conceits.
A ribcage against the light, a waterspout
fattening the lantern as it doles out Christmas cards.
I scratch, I move on, I plunge — not a single navigator left.
I touch, I turn the other cheek. Now a patter on the blinds.
A crisscross of fish between legs spread open. Scissors.
A word of advice: the balding poker deck never gave birth.
The dribbled window chews the rosebud,
its blinking in focus, the shattered glass roaming,
then the jerking, the capsized shark.
Poltroonishly, boots are scraped over stubble

The dates in these translations faithfully reproduce
Lezama's own quirky dating format.

trudging back along the sidewalk at noon.
The salamander, in a fever,
keeps leaping off the pea coat.
I can't. I'm going to bed. I'll wake up with my amulet missing.
As they spin a carpet, spiders tangle their tiny threads.
Mr. Air assembles and decapitates.

MAY & 1971 • RT

MOTHER

I saw the face of my mother again.
It was a night that seemed to have severed
night from sleep.
The night drew on or halted,
a cutting knife or a hurricane gust,
but the dream didn't head for its night.
I felt as if everything weighed upward,
you spoke there, almost murmuring,
in the ear of some tiny crab,
alright, I know this because I saw her smile
that wanted to approach to offer me
the little creature,
to watch its amusing crawl
or to plunge it in hot flour.
The ripe corncob like a baby tooth,
in a drawer teeming with silver-plated ants.
The simile of the drawer like a snake,
the size of an arm, a snake rendering slivers
out of the folded length of its tongue, the one
where old watches are kept, the hilarious
frightful talking drawer.

Groping along the door frame,
to begin to feel, covering my eyes,
though eventually motionless,
that what remained was heavier,
with the lightness of what the rain weighs
or the harp's venetian blinds.
The courtyard was attended
by the entire moon, along with the other invited meteors.
The itinerary of their habit was auspicious and magical.
I watched the door,
but the rest of her body remained subtracted,
like someone who begins to speak,
who laughs again
but who, lingering between the door
and whatever else remains,
seems to have left and then returns.
What's left is God maybe,
minus myself maybe,
maybe the solar scraping
within which, astride, maybe the self.
At my side, the other body
breathing with eyes
adhered to the rock of this spherical emptiness.
It all began to vanish
into a whirling metal with borders
assaulted by the brevity of flames,
into the steam rising from a tiny
cup of morning coffee,
into locks of hair.

MAY & 1971 · RT

UNLEASHED

The potato's humor was unleashed,
the proximity of the lettuce green
was laughing at the bottom of the sack,
followed by feigned composure
in the crumpled wrinkles of the brown paper bag.
When the alarming size of the sack
arrives with its edible stones,
it procures a pair of ghostly scissors
and starts to frolic on the rooftops.
The potato waits to be tattooed by soot,
to have its peel blessed with bruises
as they are offered by a face willing to be
devoured by smoke rising from the vulture's beak.
Despair. It's this pear, we say,
its warm wool avarice
about to begin, a beetle-browed wool
hoarding coins in the basement.
The potato came to enhance
the old concierges of Europe.
It took care of the rheumatism in their purses,
it blessed the day after tomorrow.

Skilled now, it made them
cheerfully nod this cozy secret:
the glittering tavern, a diamond at midday,
and our sweat watching gilt
proclaim its pretentious saliva.

JUNE & 1971 • RT

THE NECK

Like a rainbow-colored surge
a bottleneck
resembles the devil's throat.
A finger won't fit
and peering inside, the eye happens upon
snakes at the bottom, deepened with borage.
Like a frog,
I'm inside the bottle, my body
an Atlas between the cork
and one leg slowly surveying
its maternal foundation.
Grape and glass are related,
an undecodeable balance,
like air on the scale of Osiris.
The morning dewdrops over the grape
are like a bird's breathing:
first a bundle, then a fog-shaped body
beginning to breathe.
To uncork, the glassy eyes of a Sioux Indian,
the moment from peach fuzz against the light,
and then the waterfall surrounded by rings,

and by cries that encircle the body dictating
the new bodies stumbling
over the rocky flesh of the navel.
Inside the bottle,
one-third of a year in a damp cave,
a skeleton, a mill, a wedding:
the prison baroque.

24 JUNE & 1971 · RT

Packed with musicians,
a station wagon at midnight
rattling over old stones,
with silver filaments
like those I saw in Taxco
as I entered the city.
The comedic fat-lady
and wormy lover
fumbling with the lock
on a window — affected speech
as they pull their hair.
Shouts and bells,
the hues of a cheek
slip toward the bellowing sound
of piss relieved
by the swimming horses,
with parasols
over their swollen flanks.
Earth-tone grays
and violet flashes
boast about the rumble

deciphered by the street lamp.
With theatrical jejune,
the abandoned house
frames the musicians
who go by.
Hovering there is the apostrophe
of an arm in demand
outside the window,
crusted with frost of many feathers.
Then a grandfather clock
joins the crowd,
as it doubles over with the laughter
of each musician sinking
into his sleigh-bell pillow.
The originative tassels of time:
like the pistols drawn by Monte Cristo
or sperm-filled sacs deflated in a river.
As for the rooster?
It spread its legs
and pointed with an index finger.
And then the crackling ember
of a cigarette.

7 OCTOBER 1971 • RT

DISSONANCE

As to the contradiction of contradictions,
the contradiction of poetry,
to render the stone's reluctant reply
with a puff of smoke,
and to return to water's clarity
in search of the serene ocean chaos
severed in two: a continuity that questions,
and a rift in response,
like a hole crawling with larvae
in which, thereafter, a lobster will repose.
Its eyes tracing the carbuncular circle,
miasmas being lobsters with flaring eyes,
one half nestled in the void,
the other half clumsily scratching
the frenzy of the annotated faun.
First contradiction: to walk barefoot
over the interlacing leaves
that cover the burrows where the sun
fades like a weary sword
slashing a bonfire, newly planted.
Second contradiction: to plant bonfires.

Final contradiction: to enter
the mirror approaching us,
where backs can be viewed,
and in the likeness, eyes
begin over the eyes of leaves,
the contradiction of contradictions.
The contradiction of poetry,
effacing itself and plunging forward
with the laughable eyes of a lobster.
Each word destroys its appoggiatura
and traces a secular Roman bridge.
Each word spins in place like an affectionate
dolphin, surfacing
as faintly as a phallic prow.
Lips pursed hard when they announce
the order to retreat.
A word explodes and the sleigh dogs chew
the lanterns hanging from the trees.
As to the contradiction of contradictions,
the contradiction of poetry:
efface the letters and then inhale them at dawn
when the light effaces you.

DECEMBER & 1971 · RT

ANTHONY AND CLEOPATRA

The galleys, arms
crossed over the serpent
and the turquoise eye stained
with saffron dust.
The silky waters
contemplate with silver eyes
the embroidery furrowed along the sails
of the Roman trireme,
with a voluptuousness sweetly
scratching the holes of the flute.
Light splinters when touched
by the prow and the seagull
trembles receiving the unexpected
thrust, that like a finger tickles
the solar breast feathers
interchanging the colors of a bonfire.
The tiara slips at the level of the water
and there it mesmerizes the subdivided smile of sardines.
(Each sardine a nibble at the tiara)
(Each tiara on the volcanoes of the moon
makes a monkey in purple taffeta dance)

Tunics are billowed by the wind
when the bosom accordion keeps time.
The serpent slithers in search of a date, not a nipple,
the ringed index finger guided the bite.
The sorcerer showed the back of his leg,
he wanted to take part in the banquet
and not to read the clouds dissolving their letters.
The messenger startled by eunuchs
murmurs besides the silk galley.
At stern he is covered by an awning
of algae, Horus's nakedness
resembles death.
The ores splinter over the heads of crocodiles,
make way for the leaps
of the purple-clad monkey.
The galley halts, a crash of cymbals
in the onslaught of each wave.
The serpent leaps on the musicians' awning.
We say silk galleys
and we shut our eyes.
A millenary reminiscence
moves the serpent again, there
the nipple is reconstructed.
Regard the wood-louse walking the lettuce.

FEBRUARY & 1972 · RT

I HEAR A BIRD

I hear a speckled bird go:
caw-caw.
Three green circles inside my head
and eyes that make the night open and close.
Footstools for the violinists
and in the middle of the arabesque audacity
a carafe takes a bow as if dancing a minuet.
Prince Albert coats and moon-dappled
hats with little wings
rush to hide behind the trees.
Violins also grow severed
behind leaves stepped on by frost.
The violinist clad in a purple Prince Albert shouts:
caw-caw.
And all the drunk trombones at midnight
took their bow, pulled up the windows,
and lifted the violin's hair against the wind.
After a pause you could hear:
caw-caw.
First the animals talked,
the bird perfected the dictionary,

the orchestra made it whirl and whirl,
to release its spirals and to gather them
on the sleeve sewn with heraldic buttons.
The bird in its April long coat
offered us the intruded language,
the violin's hair crisscrossed by the silky bough,
the eye of the octopus on the midday anchor:
caw-caw.
The violinist with his angelic hair,
impelled by the orchestra and its tick-tock
of black-and-blue frost, the reverent
leaf bows again, allowing a drop
to fall hydrocephalus with bloodshot eyes:
caw-caw.

MAY & 1971 • RT

OLD SURREALIST BALLAD

When the rivulet swells with lashing
snake-tails and the piano with its backside turned
displays its shoes shining like the night
when it sinks, a sagging armchair whose old wicker
strands are still a plaything for the boy with a big head
Taking shelter from a slice of violin melon
the dancers bump their heads and perspire sawdust
and midnight is as bored
as a chessboard leaned against a blackboard
I had no plan to go, but my key chain was missing
the enormous lock the dog that always follows me
until it goes off licking the back of its leg
The violin like an arm covered with frogs
began releasing drops of evaporated honey
The chief's canoe crossed the crystal lake
at the stroke of two in the morning
and those who woke up danced with those who were sleeping
The woman we waited for is here and I hid
like a hypocrite behind a child's box of pencils
which lent me their yellow fingers
and scraps of the accordion like a grapefruit packed in syrup

I used to save tears like bread crumbs
to throw into the pool of sissified alligators
When the doughnut began to puff
the patent leather definitely squealed
and the chief's canoe was filled with crystal shards.

20 SEPTEMBER 1975 • RT

PAVILION OF NOTHINGNESS

I join the screw
posing questions in the wall,
a lackluster sound
color covered with a blanket.
But I falter and momentarily
blind, I can barely feel myself.
All at once, I call to mind,
with my fingernails I tunnel
a tokonoma in the wall.
I need a tiny hollow,
it's there I go diminishing
to reappear anew,
to touch myself and set my forehead in its place.
A tiny hollow in the wall.

Multiplier of weariness
the café I'm sitting in,
the insistent daiquiri
returning like a face of no use
for death, for springtime.
With my hands I trace the length

of a lapel that feels cold to me.
I wait for no one and I insist
on someone's pressing arrival.
All at once, with my fingernail
I draw a tiny crevice on the table.
There it is, the tokonoma, the hollow,
I'm in company unrivaled,
a corner conversation in Alexandria.
We're together in a round
of skaters through the Prado.
He was a child who inhaled
all the tenacious dew from the sky,
even then with the hollow, like a cat
that circles the whole body
with a silence full of flickerings.

Within reach of what surrounds us,
and close to our body,
the stubborn notion that says our soul
and its enwraptment fit
inside a tiny hollow in the wall
or on tissue paper scratched with a fingernail.
I'm diminishing
I'm a point that disappears and returns
and I fit full-length inside the tokonoma.
I make myself invisible
and on the verso I recover my body
swimming at the beach,
encircled by bachelors of art with banners of snow,
mathematicians and baseball players

describing sapodilla ice cream.
The hollow is smaller than a deck of cards
and it can be as big as the sky,
but we can shape it with our fingernail
along the brim of a coffee cup
or in the sky that falls beside our shoulder.

The beginning is united with the tokonoma,
in the hollow a kangaroo can hide
without forfeit of its bounding joy.
The apparition of a cave is
mysterious and begins to disentangle its dreadful.
To hide there is to tremble,
the hunter's horns resound
in the frozen forest.
But the hollow is soothing,
we can lure it with a thread
and usher it in to insignificance.
I scrape the wall with a fingernail,
slivers of lime crumble down
as though they were shards
from the celestial tortoise shell.
Is the barrenness in the hollow
the first and final path?
I fall asleep, in the tokonoma
the other still walking is the one I evaporate.

1 APRIL & 1976 • RT

CONFLUENCES (1968)

JOSÉ LEZAMA LIMA

I used to see the night as if something had fallen upon the earth, a descent. Its slowness kept me from comparing it with something descending a stair, for example. A tide upon another tide and so on, ceaselessly, until it came within reach of my feet. I would blend the falling of night with the sole expanse of the sea.

The headlights of the cars threw their beams in zigzags and the shouts of "who goes there?" began to be heard. The voices leapt from one sentry box to another. The night began to be populated, to feed and grow. From a distance, I could see it crisscrossed by ceaseless points of light. Subdivided, fragmented, riddled by the shouts and the lights. I was a long way off and could only sense the signs of its activity, like some secret parley behind closed doors in the night. Distant and voluble, mistress of its own hesitations, the night would penetrate the room where I was sleeping and I could feel how it spread through my sleep. I would rest my head on a succession of waves that reached me with their elusively slight ripples. I could feel myself resting on smoke, on a cord, between two clouds. The night gave me the gift of another skin; it must have been the night's own skin. And I would turn about in that vast skin that stretched back, as I turned, to the mossy beginnings of time.

When I was a child, I would always wait for the coming of night with undeniable terror. Terror, for me, of course, was also the room that can't be opened, the trunk with a lost key, the mirror where someone else suddenly appears beside us, a form of temptation. It was never a provocation to adventure, or a fascination on the horizon. I never rode on the back of the night as it withdrew, nor did I have to reconstruct for my other period of sleep during the day the fragments of myself that the skin of the night had left scattered separately over my bed.

The enormous skin of the night would leave me with innumerable ways of sensing for innumerable ways of evidence. The dog who during the day had passed by me many times with my hardly noticing him, now, at night, lay beside me as if asleep, and then I stared at him with the most unwavering attention. I evidence the wrinkling of his skin, the way he moves his tail and paws trying to scare off nonexistent flies. He barks in his sleep and bares his teeth angrily. In the night he has invisible enemies who still harass him. The angry reactions he had before do not now depend on anything homologous to his daytime motivations. At night he doesn't depend on motivations, but rather, unwittingly, he engenders innumerable motivations on the skin of the night that covers me.

The night has become reduced to a single point, which then grows until it becomes the night again. This reduction — which I evidence — is a hand. The placement of the hand in the night gives me a sequence of time. A time in which this can happen. The night was for me the territory where the hand could be recognized. I would say to myself: that hand can't be waiting for anything, it doesn't need any evidencing from me. And a weak voice, which must have been very far away from some small foxlike teeth, would say to me: reach out your hand and you'll see how the night and its unknown hand are there. Unknown because I could never see a body behind that other hand. Hesitant in my fear, and then inexplicably certain, I would slowly start putting out my hand, as if moving anxiously over a desert, until I found the other hand, that otherness. I would tell myself: this isn't a nightmare, go more slowly, because you may be hallucinating, but finally my hand would evidence the other hand. The conviction that it was there lessened my anguish, until my hand went back once more to being alone.

It is only now, almost half a century later, that I can clarify and even separate into different moments my nighttime quest for that other hand. My hand would fall upon it because it was waiting for me. If it hadn't been there, my failure, which would have meant another fear, of course, would have been greater than the fear engendered because the hand was there. One fear hidden inside another. Fear because the hand is there and possible fear that it might not be there.

Later, I learned that hand is also found in Rilke's *Notebooks,* and later still I learned it is found in almost all children, in almost all textbooks on child psychology.

So there already was the becoming and the archetype, life and literature, the river of Heraclitus and the unity of Parmenides. Take my hand away? Belittle my terrible experience because someone else had already suffered it too? Turn a decisive and terrible experience into a simple play of words, into literature? The time that went by taught me a solemn lesson: the conviction that what happens to us, happens to everyone. That experience of my hand upon the other hand will go on being extremely valuable, whether or not all hands held out meet all the hands of the invisible.

It was such a decisive experience that, even though it may be found in child psychology, there are still nights with that other hand, the hand that appears. There will always be a night when the other hand comes and other nights when my hand remains rigid and unvisited.

I waited not only for the other hand but also for the other word, the word that is always forming in us a continuum that for a few moments is created and then destroyed. A flower that forms another flower when a dragonfly comes to rest on it. To know that for a few moments something comes to complete us, and that by breathing more deeply we find a universal rhythm. A breathing in and breathing out that are a universal rhythm. Things hidden are things that complete us and make a plenitude in the length of their waves. The knowing that is not ours and the not knowing that is ours form for me true knowledge.

The word in the moments of its hypostasis, the complete body behind the word, the syllable, the wrinkling of someone's lips or the unexpected irregularity in someone's eyebrows. The residue left in each word by the vast dimensions of the stars became a momentary mirror. A fine sand that left letters, indications. A solitary word that became a prayer. Words were a hand excessive in its perspiration, an adjective was someone's profile or head-on look, eyes upon eyes, with the tension of a deer's perked-up ears.

Every word was for me the innumerable presence of that fixity of the hand in the night. "It's time for a bath," "let's have lunch now," "off to bed," "someone's at the door" were for me like inscriptions that engendered ceaseless evaporations, unchanging and obsessive sketches for novels. They were *larvae* developing into metaphors in continuous chains, like a farewell and then another visit.

Waiting for the hand and having it come would start the verbal chain, or in that unending development the nighttime hand would be found. Sometimes waiting for the hand was fruitless and that would disproportionately separate one syllable from another, one word from its traveling companion. It was a momentary void because of the distance, which could engender things either in an anxious time of waiting or in the paradoxical emptiness of some good advice. It was like a move made in a game that fell, or I should say *collapsed,* upon some unknown board. A disturbing verbal move, because something advanced and then something in return offered a challenge and sent out its call over a net that brought up only one single fish eager to befriend all others.

In this way, I found in every word a germ that sprang from a union of the most distant stars with the most hidden things inside us, just as, at the end of time, the pause and expansion of each moment of our breathing will be occupied by an irreplaceable and unique word. In each word there will be a germ planted in the communicating vessels of the sentence, but in that world the verbal germ, as in the succession of visible and invisible spaces in breathing, produces the astonishment natural to man at a coordinate in time. The realm of the stars, that realm the Taoists called the silent sky, required the transmutations in man's deepest flesh, the fires of his innermost organs, his most secret inner changes, for the purposes of which the mysterious pineal eye perhaps existed, the extinct inner mirror reconstructed by the Greeks as "being," like the *moi haïssable* of Pascal, like the "unified self" of the Alexandrines, which later will attain its highest expression in Saint Augustine's *logos spermatikos,* the participation of each individual word in the universal word, a participation that includes a breathing that joins the visible and the invisible, a metamorphic digestion and a spermatic processional that changes the germ into a universal word, a complementary protoplasmatic hunger that engenders the participation of each and every word in an infinite, recognizable possibility.

But man not only germinates, he also elects. I would stress the similarity between these two phenomena, which are for me equally mysterious, because when we elect we start a new germ, but, since this germ stands in a more direct relation to man, we will call it an "act." In the dimension of poetry, to carry out an act and to elect are like a prolongation of the germ, because that act and that election come within what is known as the tactile consciousness of the blind, though, even as I venture to call it that, I know I only slightly approximate what it is.

It is an act that takes place and an election that occurs in a ciphered form beyond nature, in supernature. The answer to a question that cannot be formulated, that floats in infinity. A ceaseless answer to the terrible question posed by the demiurge: Why does it rain in the desert? Act and election that take place in supernature. Cities that man reaches and then cannot reconstruct. Cities slowly built over thousands of years and then struck down and leveled in the blink of an eye. Made and unmade with the rhythm of our breathing. Sometimes made by the sudden descent of the stars and other times made like a row of instantaneous columns rising out of the earth.

What is "supernature"? The penetration of the image into nature engenders supernature. In that dimension I never tire of repeating the words of Pascal, which were a revelation for me: "since true nature has been lost, everything can be nature"; the terrible affirmative force of those words made me decide to put the image in the place of the nature that has been lost. In that way, man replies to the determinism of nature with the total freedom of the image. And the pessimism of lost nature is answered with the invincible joy in man of the reconstructed image.

Do they live in some ruins? Are they actors on vacation? Is there a painter there? We are looking at Goya's painting *La gruta,* one of his best but one of his least considered. In the background, the purple sky and accumulated clouds of El Greco, contrasting with the calm flight of the doves. Covered by the tablecloth, or underneath the table, they hide so the pigeons will come closer. A coliseum in ruins, a deserted square, the collapsed wing of a convent. In front of that desolation they have set up a stall to sell food, where an apparition covered with a tablecloth pecked by the pigeons engenders expectation and humor. It is an unknown space and an errant time that have no place on earth. And yet, we walk in this here and elapse in this now, and we succeed in reconstructing an image. That is supernature.

Supernature is revealed not only by man's intervention in nature: man and nature both, each at their own risk, join together in supernature. Among the Tartars, dead children marry. On fine paper, drawings are made of the warriors who attend the wedding, the musicians, the family members bearing pitchers for the libations. All those present sign their names and the signatures are kept in well-guarded archives. Both families of the dead children try to keep each other company, living in the same neighborhood. They share their property and celebrate all ritual feasts together. Here we have life going on very actively around the dead and the dead children as a couple penetrating life. This is a reply to what the morphologists of the Goethean school have claimed, that all species in becoming more perfect engender a new species, in the same way that nature, when enlarged by the image man provides, attains to the new realm of supernature.

In the *mastabas* of ancient Egypt, a door was always left open to receive the magnetic winds of the desert. Genetic winds that the dead continue to receive. The penetration of the pyramids northward into the parched lands caused the queen's chamber to be constructed with the most favorable orientation possible for receiving the magnetic winds of the genesial desert. Hence my belief that the construction of the pyramids was meant to create not only a lasting space for the dead but also a genesial chamber for the kings to procreate with the concurrence of the magnetic winds of the desert. In this way a true lineage of both dead and living kings was attained. One after another the pyramids advanced into the parched lands, into the region of the dead, just as the humus, the muddy lands, were inhabited by the living, and so, at the very edge of death, the genesial chamber of the queen received the plenitude of the magnetic winds, to which Baudelaire's elastic phantoms, the cats considered godlike by Egyptian culture, are so sensitive.

For the Egyptians, the only talking animal was the cat, who could speak the word "like" that could join together the two magnetic ends of its whiskers. These two magnetic points, infinitely relatable to one another, lie at the basis of all metaphorical analogies. It is a genesial, copulative relatedness. Join together the magnetic points of a hedgehog with those of a shepherd's pouch, an example we are very fond of, and a chestnut is engendered. The magnetic "like" also awakens new species and the realm of supernature.

Supernature has little to do with the *proton pseudos,* the poetic lie of the Greeks, since supernature never loses the primordial substance from which it comes, because it joins the one to the nondual one, and since man is image, participates in the world as such and in the end encounters a total clarification of the image. If the image were denied him then he would have no knowledge whatsoever of resurrection. The image is the unending complement to what we can only partly see and hear. Pascal's fearful *entredeux* can only be filled by the image.

Horror vacui is the fear of being left with no images at all, in times when the pessimistic combinational finitude of separate particles prevailed over the demiurge's spiraling movement to break away. In numerous medieval legends there are mirrors that do not reflect the image of a damaged or demoniacal body, because when the mirror does not speak, the devil sticks out his slimy tongue. That innate conviction in man of knowing that our key can open the door of another house, our sword can lead another army in the desert, our cards can play another game in another place. Everywhere there is the reminiscence of something unconditioned and unknown to us, a reminiscence engendered by a causality in what we can see, which we sense like a lost city we recognize anew. Actually, everything the image is based upon is hypertelic, goes beyond its finality, rejects that finality, and offers the infinite surprise of what I have called "the ecstasy of participation in the homogeneous," a point, an image, ranging in space. It is a tree, a reminiscence, a conversation strengthening a river by tracing a line with our finger.

Germ, act, and then potency. Possibility of the act, the act upon a point, and a point that resists. The point is an Argus, a lynx, and leaves its track among the stars. Its traces, endowed with an invisible phosphorescence, are lasting. In all this there is a finite possibility that potency interprets and develops. A man's act can reproduce a germ in nature, and make poetry permanent by a secret relationship between germ and act. It is a germ-act that man can accomplish and reproduce. The howling, penetrating unity of a hunt, a cry of exultation, the permanent response of an orchestra in time, the warriors in the shadow of the walls of Ilium, the *Grande Armée,* what I have called the imaginary eras and also supernature — all these form by an interaction of germ, act, and potency new and unknown germs, acts, and potencies. Planting a germ or seed on earth also means planting it among the stars, and following the course of a river also means walking one's way through the clouds, just as in Chinese theater a certain movement of the legs signifies riding on horseback.

When potency is applied to a point or when it acts in space, it does so always in company with the imago, the deepest unity we can know between the realm of the stars and the earth. If potency were to act without the image, it would be only a self-destructive act having no participation, but every act, every potency, is an infinite growth, an overriding excess, in which the stars reinforce the earth. The image, in participating in the act, produces a momentary visibility, which, without the image as the only recourse available to man, would be an impenetrable excess. In that way, man takes over that excess, makes it come forth and reincorporates a new excess. All *poiesis* is an act of participation in that excess, a participation of man in the universal spirit, in the Holy Spirit, in the universal mother.

Man as germ points to that development in his surroundings, and a broad strong basic trunk equates it with a fervor for establishing foundations, though we will never know, looking only at nature, what causal series produce splendor or decay, nor at what moment the unconditioned will irresistibly penetrate into those causal series. In some Asian cities, when people move from life into death, the dead are not taken out through the door, but instead a wall is torn down, as if the dead were being prepared for a new order of causality. In other Asian cities, at the moment of cremation, drawings on paper made by friends, and jewels and food are also put into the flames, as if to provide protection and company during a voyage that is supposed to be into another space.

In a few chosen vessels, as they are called in the Bible, their development in life goes forward along with a prodigious anticipation of that other space. From the stark plains of Castille comes the foundation established by Saint Teresa as an oblique experience that is later reproduced in Martí, for whom the paradoxical germ of exile takes the place of the desert. After his imprisonment, Martí must have felt a kind of rebirth in the image of resurrection, just as later, after his death, he comes forth again in our flesh. The desert and its new symbolic appearance in an exile become equivalent. Hence, in *Paradiso*, in order to prepare the way for his last encounter with Oppiano Licario, in order to attain to the new causality, to the Tibetan city, José Cemí has to go through all the occurrences and recurrences of the night. The placental descent of night, the balancing point of midnight, appear as variants of desert and exile. All the possibilities of the poetic system have been set in motion, so that Cemí can keep his appointment with Licario, the Icarus, the new attempter of the impossible.

In *Paradiso*, world outside time becomes equivalent to supernature, since time is also lost nature and the image is reconstructed as supernature. Liberation from time is the most unrelenting constant of supernature. Oppiano Licario wants to provoke that supernature. Thus he continues on its quest through ceaseless labyrinths. Chapter 12, negation of time: inside the glass urn the dead boy and the dead centurion ceaselessly exchange faces. But in chapter 14, at the end, the one who appears in the urn is Oppiano Licario himself. Negation of time achieved in sleep, where not only time but also space disappear. I move the enormity of an ax, I reach infinite velocities, I see the blind men in the markets at night talking about the pictorial qualities of strawberries, and finally the Roman soldiers playing dibstones in the ruins: I attain the tetractis, the number four, god. Chapter 13 attempts to show a *perpetuum mobile* in order to break free of spatial conditioning. The sheep's head turning on a pinion attains that freedom and in that dimension of Oppiano Licario, the dimension of supernature, the figures from a childhood past return. It is a cognitive infinity acquired in Licario's presence, but in a different Pythagorean rhythm: from the systaltic, violent rhythm of the passions, there has been a movement to the hesichastic rhythm of tranquility and contemplative wisdom.

Licario has set in motion the vast coordinates of his poetic system in preparation for his last encounter with Cemí. It was necessary for Cemí to have his last encounter with Licario's words. "The spider and the image in place of the body" is one of the statements he is given on the last night. Licario's sister Inaca Eco Licario appears and delivers that poetic statement as if it were a promised land. The shadow, the double, is the one who delivers the offering. The double makes the first offering, delivers the first image, and Cemí ascends the sacrificial stone in order to put into effect his patronymic meaning of "idol" or "image." Let us suppose a starry Pythagorean night in 1955. I have spent several hours listening to Johann Sebastian's *Art of the Fugue,* absorbed in the interweavings of the *juga per canon.* Infinite relationships are attained in the spirals of the night. The constructions and dilations of the rhythm are repeated in each of our steps and we grow as we walk. We go down one of those streets that have swollen like the rivers of paradise. The lights of the funeral parlor shining in the night, without realizing it, have to startle and halt the person walking by. The repeated music of a merry-go-round sustains and hastens the person on a nighttime stroll. The house in its vertical dimension, like a demented tree, thrusts at us the temptation of its last terrace, where, under the protection of the priapic god Terminus, two buffoons are playing chess. Here there is something like the repetition of a circular movement. At the very edge of death, the coordinates of the poetic system thrash about desperately; with nature now exhausted, supernature subsists; with the earthly image now shattered, the unending stellar images begin. There, in the most unattainable distance, where the Pythagoreans located the soul of the stars.

The surprise is the house with its blinding lights, which the man interprets, while his saliva thickens and the circulations of his lymph and blood flow together. A *maestoso* and a *vivace* form a new unity that moves forward like a chessman into the invisible. In the merry-go-round there is also a circular repetition that breaks into spirals, into a shower of stars in the Babylonian night, into the comet that precedes and announces the death of Julius Caesar. A black cat of enormous size that goes from one crowd of people to another, as an announcement of death. The searching orange spheres in Van Gogh's night, cast like stones into the belly of the whale. It is the secret conversation at the entrance to Toledo in El Greco. It is the infinitely repeated music of the merry-go-round, between the blazing house of death and the infinite vertical polyhedron, where the image would like to set up its winter quarters. It is the indomitable urge to reach the Tibetan city of the stars, where man converses with the white buffalo, where vegetal shadows penetrate our sleep. One day I heard one of our *decimistas* say, as he turned an octosyllable: "the soul grows in the shade" *(el alma se da en la sombra)*. An intuition that concurs with a theologian who tells us that man has to feel like the plants, think like the angels, and live like the animals. Perhaps, at the other end of the cord occupied by the angel, what we have is not the beast, but rather that happy coincidence of humanism's *otium cum dignitate* and the grazing of the beasts, both of which are manifestations of the Taoist's contemplation of the silent sky. The day we can establish a mutual clarification between human leisure and animal grazing, true nature will again be inhabited, because in both activities there is an expectation of the realm of the stars, of the world of infinite openness, for the complete relationship between animals and their surroundings has not yet been deeply understood and we are still ignorant of how the interrelationships of the universal word are established, but some day the world of *gnosis* and the world of *physis* will be univocal.

A surprise in the course of the seasons. Rain and more rain. When we go to bed, the cold linen offers its first rebuff, we have to press the pillow closer to our cheek to feel the delight of resting against something, a sensation like sailing into a resistance that can be overcome. Our sleep, as it continues, occupies new fragments of the night. Wool at night, slowly and secretly, comes to prevail over daytime linen, and the goat goes on dancing, but no longer in the sunbeam. All that is hidden, closed off, put away, opens its doors and offers the quiet new sumptuousness of a new marketplace. Cotton coins that make no metallic sound purchase magical fabrics. Shapeless forms that had been kept in the storehouse now move toward the four bonfires blazing at the four corners of the marketplace and turn into clusters of faces. All that is hidden and dark, as the new season arrives, takes on figure and shape, becomes the child who leaves his house every morning in Whitman's poem. And he comes back and tells his tale. And he gets lost and goes on with his tale: Can you hear him?

In the big house on the army base, I used to watch the coming of winter. The kitchen, the dining room, and the bedrooms became more subtle in their differences, their silences made a more inward sound, conversations turned more to whispers. My grandmother would visit us more often. Our preparations for her visits were very extensive and careful; it seemed as if she were coming to spend the whole winter with us, but the day after she arrived, at breakfast we would hear her say: "I don't like to abandon my house on the Prado," using the word "abandon" the way a queen refers to a castle that has been abandoned or the way we refer to a neighbor who has abandoned her children. An abandonment and neglect grandmother found intolerable. She would spend a very happy day with us, but by late afternoon she was already getting ready to go back home. I would spend the rest of the day in the sadness of that farewell. I would wander much too slowly through every room in the house. I would linger as I went from the living room out to the backyard and see there, hung out for airing, the bedspreads that were going to inaugurate the winter. Somebody would come and start beating the dust out of the bedspreads with some long branches. And the dust flying up would turn into showers of sparks that enlarged or blotted out the faces that would come out of the fabric until the branches made them disappear. On misty winter days I liked to watch those faces that only my imago projected and that then faded away, sneezing from the dust.

Those faces I attempted to fix in a poem:

Golpea el pastor con su cayado
las más delgadas telas,
después del inútil ruido del azoro,
otra llamada, que ya no está, nos viene.
Ese ruido, naciendo en otra puerta,
se deshace en las preguntas de una muerte.
Ruido de otro total se perdería,
si no fuese universal la caras de la tela.
Nadando en nuestro instante alguien viene
a brindar su cuello por regusto o sucesión
y aunque el cayado se aplaque por las venas,
saca, saca las caras de la tela.
El golpe no es el que corresponde a cada cara
y cada cara se pierde por la tela.

The shepherd knocks with his staff
the thinnest fabrics,
after the useless noise of the fright,
another call, not there any more, comes to us.
That noise, arising at another door,
dissolves into the questions of a death.
Noise of another total would be lost,
if the flesh of the fabric were not universal.
Swimming in our instant someone comes
to offer his neck in aftertaste or succession

and even though the staff is placated in the veins,
it brings, brings out the faces from the fabric.
The knock is not the one that corresponds to each face
and each face is lost in the fabric.

But the poem was also imparted by a kind of daring. Its title taken
from esoteric Pythagorean thought and symbolic mathematics was
pervaded by another adolescent innocence. The poem was accompa-
nied by another memory, not the clouds of autumn, but the operations
of algebra. Things hidden behind the full moon of the zero. A negative
quantity coming to strengthen another growth in memory. In that
winter fabric, behind those clouds of dust, there were chubby-faced
angels or bony heads nodding and oozing tar and pitch. Remember
that figures appearing in showers of sparks, billowing dust, or clouds
display obvious traces of pitch on their teeth, their fingertips, or their
earlobes: Are these perhaps the signs of their origin or derivation?
Unknown affinities with the world of carbon and flames are betrayed
at times, and this makes the figures recognizable, because of their
blackheads or the dust left on them from their conversations with
María la Luna.

Hidden in the minus zero, in the layers of dust, the faces kept on
disappearing. When the branches began to beat the bedspreads, the
signs would dig their nails into the negative quantities in order to
hang on to a few faces, a few intersecting lines, until finally the fabric
was alive with conversations, with after-dinner talk, with inter-
changeable faces. It seemed as if the masks were kept in huge ward-
robes with three mirrors and came back from one season to another.

The house offered not only that expected metamorphosis but also
continuing hidden marvels. The colonel's study. Tables with maps
and drawings, weapons hanging on the wall, diplomas, medals, armil-

lary spheres, Mercator projections. That was located on the other side of our parents' bedroom, beyond which we never went. The "beyond" was the study, where the colonel spent most of his afternoons and evenings. If we ever penetrated that room, through some furtively opened door, we would then run away in fright, like someone who has entered an atmosphere that refracts him. We would go in slowly, looking at a corner or a shadow or a creaking piece of furniture, and then run out like arrows shot from a bow.

That room was also a gift from the course of the seasons. It would be opened up to the curiosity of the other inhabitants of the house in the muffled passage from summer to winter. There you could see a piece of black and green marble, comparative drawings of daggers from Florence and Berlin, an obsidian chess set with men as large as your hand. It would be opened up simply to be aired out, but for us it was a kind of magic spell, a challenge, something that invited us to commit some exceptional act and then withdraw in concealment. Those figures appearing in the changes of seasons, those fleeting sallies beyond what we ordinarily knew, occurred slowly, as if lingeringly and apart from any repetition. Insistence did not seem to be part of their nature. They were fleeting, barely glimpsed, shadowy, but how deeply they satisfied us, and now that we are separated from ourselves by the dusty sands of time, they seem as if they had been repeated over and over again, as if innumerable faces kept coming out of the fabrics, as if we had made whole sojourns out beyond the Pillars of Hercules.

From that room, library, storeroom, resting place for wayward things, I would later unravel the magic that I have sensed in all dwelling places of men, like the protectiveness of a snail that offers its defensive labyrinths to the assaults of the ocean's waves in the darkness of night.

It was the conviction that there, in the remoteness of what was right at hand, could be found all the sparks of an unseen forge. All the inhabitants of the house were asleep, but in that room that was unlike the others, we could perceive the difference with all the secret involutions of our being; there were movements so slow as to extend over thousands of years or centered on a wheel spinning with dizzying speed. There life took on indecipherable movements, remnants of some liturgy in a deserted forest or dense filterings down into some underwater cave, but the sleepers would come holding their tiny seashells to listen to the stars and broad lecterns would allow the intoning of psalms.

The conviction that the dragon, what is there and not there, what appears and disappears, needs a place of protection out beyond the Pillars of Hercules, also had at its disposal the library as a supernature. There, in solitude one seeks company, and more specifically in public libraries, where company seeks solitude. The struggle against the dragon had to take place in the ceaseless relationships between solitude and company. From the memory of the mysterious room, out beyond the pillars, on the army base, would come my conception of Chinese culture: the library as dragon. Lao-tzu, he of the sense of the creative that is uncreated, was a librarian, and Doctor Kung Tse, the Confucius of the Jesuits, spent the last fourteen years of his life working on the *I Ching,* the book of changes, of the visible and the invisible, where the dragon takes up lodging in a book to speak with the dead and trace the coordinates between the insignificant and the vast excess of the stars. And, just as we can make writing more legible with fire, so we can speak with the invisible.

In itself, the urge to bring to a book that which cannot be heard or seen, the urge to have the uncreated that creates take on meaning, tells us that the struggle with the dragon has to be out beyond the pillars, that it will be in an imaginary era, that it will have its place in super-nature. And just as it is claimed in some medieval legend that the devil likes to sleep in the shadow of the bell tower, so the uncreated that creates likes to spend the day in the library, because the library has begun by being something unheard, unseen, and thus nature will be found again in supernature.

We have also lost the living sense of things so decisive for man as a bonfire, a glass of water, a mirror, or a sword, or as the alphabet, that safeguard to keep caravans from being lost in the desert. Along with the memory of the house, the river, the planted fields, the bull, in the alphabet we find the five letters that poetry provides. These are signs that cannot be deciphered; they must not be signs of reminiscences of figures, but symbols of the persistence of the secret challenge concentrated in an alphabet. This is the offering made by poetry, five unknown letters, wayward analogue between the stars and the earth, of the cloud entering the mirror. These were the letters in the depths that leap out like fish when we drink water from our cupped hands.

I would look out into the backyard again and that distance between the limits of the house and the line of the horizon also became filled with unknown figures. The presence of hand upon hand in the middle of the night would change into a column of army mules going down into the woods, into the darkness. I would watch them and see how, with the most invincible resistance, they moved into a destiny they knew nothing about. They plodded their way through Fall and Redemption, enduring total sorrow. The closer I got to them, the more clearly I could see the trembling of their skin. They would sweat, tremble, and plod, on and on. They knew nothing of their destiny, but they resisted. They went down into their Fall as into their Glory, and their resistance lighted the way for the passage of great transports. One might say that in reply to the punishment they receive they offer the punishment of their resistance. They move unknowingly out beyond the pillars, breathe like bellows in supernature, and move the broad foundations of imaginary eras. Their distances are occupied by the ceaseless transformations of poetry. The resistance of the mule sows its seeds in the abyss, just as the duration of poetry sows its seeds by a resurgence in the stars. The one resists in its body, the other resists in time, and the incipient wings of each can be seen to seek their complements, unknown, known, and again unknown.

Because of an unprecedented increase in collections of family photographs, I realized that I was moving from a blazing zenith, from the ways of the *splendor formae,* down into a deep darkness. When my mother died, her album of family pictures enlarged my collection. In hers the people most frequently depicted were those who had gone down into the shadows of Hades, whereas in mine it was my contemporaries, those who still enjoyed the realm of light. What I can now contemplate with apparent calm was for me then a very violent, desperate shock. It was as if old relationships, the most pathetic family stories, had become peopled anew, had come to the table after dinner and could quietly dialogue with us, without the slightest alarm on our part.

Amid all these dizzying trials, I found myself plunged into darkness. The more these pictures found their places in the reaches of the past, the more they took on for me the dim glow of words read under a gas lamp. These portraits regained their serene joy, their sumptuous presence. They were real ghosts, tangibly existing in the image that provided them with bodies to walk about in, with voices that could be heard, and with deeply moving farewells. The image they had abandoned like an egg embodied them anew. They lived in the palace with the green windows, went about the city with a hundred doors, came to hear mass in the Cathedral of Havana. That exquisite and most refined group of people, never complaining, never hurried, did not need any help from me to reach the house where the dragon was lodged. I am the spirit befuddled by those apparently confused emigrants, I am the one who listens, seeks, and brings together again the cotton and the scent of vanilla, the wavering lamp and the ancestral yellow of the lace. There stands Andresito, the child prodigy, holding his violin: he was killed in an accident in a benefit held to collect funds for the cause of Cuban Independence. He was playing that night in the tuxedo his father often wore. He fell from the elevator and died and my grandfather died soon after of grief. And my grandmother, telling the story of it all, would end with a kind of antistrophe from some Greek tragedy: And why did it have to be my son? When I was a child I wanted to be that violinist, the one who would attain expression in exchange for a confrontation with the *fatum*. He was constantly configured in me, even across the distance of death. He was the absent one, gone with the best of the family into the darkness of Moira, taking up all our family *simpathos,* and I liked to hear my grandmother and my mother tell what his studies and the night he died were like. And the delicacy of my Aunt Queta, my father's sister, secretly in love with my Uncle Alberto, my mother's brother, who, beneath his exterior as the ne'er-do-well uncle that all families have, possessed the treasure of a style of conversation that I have always sought to have as the source of my own stories.

In 1880 my maternal grandfather, who was very Cuban and who went into revolutionary exile years later, made a trip to Spain. Around the same time, my paternal grandfather, who was a Basque and very Spanish, made his trip to Cuba. Years after, both families entwined their destinies in such a way that whenever I have been called a *vasco criollo* I have always felt a special pride, but my true pride I need not even confess.

A few years before she died, my grandmother opened up a gigantic wardrobe that was located in the back room of her Prado house, and then my youthful years felt a great flood of memories rush over me. There were my grandfather's tuxedo, the one my Uncle Andresito died in, and the dresses that my grandmother had worn to all her daughters' weddings. There also was an enormous inkstand with an inkwell and some solid silver reindeers, and lying on top of the inkstand was an amber backscratcher of the kind often used in the eighteenth and nineteenth centuries. That innocent wave of recollections went into the second stanza of my poem "Oda a Julián del Casal," where, to suggest the title of one of Casal's own poems, I allude to the reindeer on the inkstand and an amber backscratcher. Sometimes I think with delight that on the day of farewells, that gigantic wardrobe will again open for me. We hear once more:

> *Déjenlo que acompañe sin hablar,*
> *permitidle, blandamente, que se vuelva*
> *hacia el frutero donde están los osos*
> *con el plato de nieve, o el reno*
> *de la escribanía, con su manilla de ámbar.*

> Let him be with us and not speak,
> allow him, softly, to turn
> toward the fruit bowl where the bears are
> with the plate of snow, or the reindeer
> on the inkstand, with its amber backscratcher.

It was a prayer I was saying for Casal and for myself.

Inside that magic wardrobe, Uncle Andresito's violin, protected from the dust in its tightly closed case, displayed the silent veins in its wood. Streaks of amber, small tomb of jasper, tiny graceful citadel erected by Amphion. In those parades in my poem "Pensamientos en la Habana," where I don't want to choose my shoes in a store window, where I indicate that the scratch on the lute deciphers nothing, where I conjecture that the first flute was made from a stolen branch, suddenly there comes "the violin of ice shrouded in recollection" *(el violín de hielo amortajado en la reminiscencia),* which awakens the forest harmonium that ties and unbraids the strands of memory. And it is the violin that seems to exhale the poem's final orchestration: "my soul is not in an ashtray" *(mi alma no está en un cenicero).*

An ancient legend of India reminds us there is a river whose tributaries cannot be known. In the end its flow becomes circular and begins to boil. A tremendous confusion can be seen as it sweeps along, things totally unlike and trivial coexist with jewel-like symmetries and harmonious love. This is the Puraná, carrying everything in its waters, always seeming to be in confusion, with no analogue or likeness possible. And yet this is the river that leads to the gates of Paradise. Amid the reflections of its waves pass in procession the potter's vestibule, the tree of coral, the chain of the tiger's eye, the celestial Ganges, the malachite terrace, the hell of the lances and the repose of the perfect man. A ceaseless contemplation of the river transmits its dualism, the adventure of the analogue and the couples who retire to their small islands. A tree before certain eyes, a tree of coral before the tiger's eye; the lances before the terrace, and then the infernal lances before the paradisiacal terrace of malachite. Blessed are we the ephemeral who can contemplate movement as an image of eternity and follow intently the parabola of the arrow until it is buried beneath the line of the horizon.

· JI ·

INTERVIEW WITH
JOSÉ LEZAMA LIMA (1964)

ARMANDO ALVAREZ BRAVO

ARMANDO ALVAREZ BRAVO: You are known and renowned as an enigmatic poet. For many you are the figure of obscurity par excellence in Cuban poetry. There is no doubt that your endeavor inaugurates a novel way of seeing things that delivers nothing easily to the reader and instead demands of him an alert attitude. After these twenty-five years, how do you consider what has been said and is still said about these characteristics of your poetry?

JOSÉ LEZAMA LIMA: I do not think that the contemplation of my poetry offers at present greater difficulty than that offered by the contemplation of any other poetic prism. It is true that our romantic and later our fin-de-siècle poetry had no elements that could be considered enigmatic. But this fact cannot serve to join together, as is customary, the concepts of the enigmatic and the obscure. These two concepts are not necessarily tangent. Once I was told that Góngora was a poet who made clear things obscure and that I, on the contrary, was a poet who made obscure things clear, obvious, radiant. I have stressed the fact that it was among medieval minstrels that the *trobar clus* appeared, these being the minstrels who produced obscure poetry. Thus we see that even minstrelsy, which by definition was simple, had nothing to do with clarity, since already among the minstrels there were some who produced obscure or hermetic poetry. And in Nordic countries there were kings who were skalds that in their own palaces cultivated obscure poetry, just as there were kings who performed as buffoons in their own courts. The verses of the skalds were always nebulous and difficult to understand. For example:

> I place the round serpent
> on the tongue of the falcon's perch
> beside the bridge of Odin's shield.

What this means is that a ring is placed on the small finger of the hand. One needs to know that falcon's perch means the falconer's hand. The tongue is the small finger. And the bridge of Odin's shield is the arm from which the warrior's shield hangs. It is told that a skald, a hermetic Nordic troubadour, invited a king to have some beer soup. The monarch accepted, and the poet took him to the edge of the ocean, where he said: there's your soup; when you finish, you'll have your beer. I cite these examples taken from skalds so you can see that obscure poetry has nothing to do with the baroque, with the dazzling baroque of Marino, of Chiabrera, of Góngora. There is obscure poetry and there is clear poetry.

This is a fact that we have to accept simply, just as we accept the existence of the day and of the night, of the things that are done by day and the things that are done by night. But you will understand, my friend, that, in short, neither are obscure things so obscure as to terrify us, nor are clear things so clear as to let us sleep in peace. But all this business about obscurity and clarity now seems to me outmoded, overworked. What matters is what Pascal called *pensées de derrière*.

That is, the eternally enigmatic other side of things, both of the obscure or distant and of the clear and immediate. The tendency toward obscurity, toward resolving enigmas, toward playing games within games, is as common to humankind as is our image reflected in the clear surface of the water, which can lead us with egotistical voluptuousness to the final blow, to our death. There is no need to seek obscurities where they do not exist.

ARMANDO ALVAREZ BRAVO: Image in your poetry is a motif, a theme, a concern. It arises as a defense against realities that become realities by their own momentum, but, at the same time, it arises as a force. How do you establish the relationships between image and metaphor?

JOSÉ LEZAMA LIMA: In the terms of my poetic system of the world, metaphor and image have as much in the way of carnality or living flesh within the poem as they have in the way of philosophical efficacy, external world, or essential reason. One of the mysteries of poetry is the relationship between the analogue or connective force of metaphor, which advances and by so doing creates what we might call the substantive ground of poetry, and this advance through infinite analogies to a final point where the image is located, which image has a powerful regressive force, capable of covering all that substantiveness. The relation between metaphor and image can be likened to a horse that can both fly and swim and persists within a resistant substance, which is what we may consider the image to be. The image is the reality of the invisible world. Thus the Greeks placed images as populators of the world of the dead. I believe that the marvel of a poem is that it manages to create a body, a resistant substance set between a metaphor that advances by creating infinite connections and a final image that assures the survival of that substance, that *poiesis*. In the same way that man has created orchestras, battles, soldiers sleeping in the shadow of palisades, great armadas, and homes in the bellies of whales, he has also created artificial bodies that are both caressable and resistant, like nature itself eluding and yielding to our touch. Once, when I was speaking of Martí and trying to establish the mysterious laws of poetry (and don't forget that the first laws were written in poetic form), I made reference to the fact that for those prodigious laws of the imagination twenty years of absence are equivalent to a sudden vortex in death, just as, in an orchestra, a trumpet may be equivalent to twenty violins. The connections of metaphor are progressive and infinite. The firecovering that the image forms over the substantiveness of poetry is as unitary and fixed as a star. That's why I state in one of my poems this deep paradox of poetry: that love is not made caressingly from pore to pore, but from pore to star, where space forms a suspension and the body plunges down and swims at length.

ARMANDO ALVAREZ BRAVO: When you reached your mature years you set forth a very personal conception of poetry, a poetic system. The formulation of this system began to take shape in a series of prose fragments included in your book of poems *La fijeza* (1949). What we might classify as theory had its beginnings as poetry. Those first insights later took on a discursive form in essays and the bases of the system were nurtured from different sources. In spite of this later evolution, is it still correct to think that the driving force of the system is fundamentally poetic?

JOSÉ LEZAMA LIMA: That's correct. The driving force is essentially poetic. Some innocent people, terrified by the word *system,* have thought my system is a philosophical study *ad usum* of poetry. Nothing could be further from my intention. I have always proceeded on the basis of elements proper to poetry, that is, poem, poet, metaphor, image. When I began to come of age intellectually — and like all poets I have been a man of varied and voluptuous readings, following the tradition of La Fontaine, who postulated the poet as the *amateur de toutes les choses, le polyphile,* I came to understand that, by virtue of that hazardous and reversible play of metaphor and image, what seemed to be a dispersion in my readings was really an all-devouring urge toward integration into a unity, into a mirror, into a water both flowing and fixed. One day I was thinking about great periods of history that have had neither great nor powerful poets and yet were great periods for the world of poetry. It was a very important fact for me that, from Lucretius and Virgil down to the appearance of Dante, there had been no great poets in that immense expanse of time, no access to the poet as an expressive unity. And these were the times of Charlemagne, of the *Enchiridion* or Magic Book, the cathedrals, the Holy Grail, the knights of King Arthur, the Crusades, the Golden Legend, Saint Francis, Saint Catherine. . . . This led me to study what I call the imaginary eras or eras dominated by an image, which I have expounded in several essays that I believe are the most significant part of my work.

ARMANDO ALVAREZ BRAVO: I would like you to tell me more about those imaginary eras. And, within them, about how conceptions that are pagan from your own Catholic point of view can be integrated into Christian conceptions, producing thereby a denial of Heidegger's postulate of man as a creature destined for death and offering instead, as you do in your system, a postulate of man as a creature destined for resurrection by way of poetry.

JOSÉ LEZAMA LIMA: For me it is both fascinating and difficult to speak about all that you suggest. The subject offers infinite possibilities. I see it all as a whole, and it is impossible for me to express it in a moment, or perhaps even in an eternity, as such. Whenever I approach it I come up against this difficulty, but let us talk. There is an Idumaean period, or period of phallic fabulation, when the human being is still joined to the vegetal and when time, because of hibernation, does not have the meaning it later takes on for us. In each of man's metamorphoses, his dormancy creates a fabulous time. Thus, there appears the mysterious tribe of Idumaea, in Genesis, in which reproduction is not based on carnal dialogue by couples, on germinal dualism. The human being falls asleep on the cool riverbanks, beneath the broad foliage of the trees, and with graceful slowness a tree sprouts from his shoulder. The man goes on sleeping and the tree goes on growing, thickening its bark and roots and moving closer to the secret mobility of the river. This new creature of the germinating tree detaches itself in the propitious season of summer and smilingly begins to sing its rowing songs in the dawn of the rivers. This is how man lived, close to primitive nebulas and the trees, which, as they grew, gained perspectives with no need to be submissive in movement. This is the great period when the evidence of beauty is immediate. But there are others. We can refer to the presence of the image in the siege of Ilium, whose reality is preserved by poetry in the face of its dark destruction. Or the relationship between the mysteries of the priest kings and Fou Hi (2697 B.C.) preserved in texts like the *Tao Te Ching,* a title whose closest translation might be "The Book of the Creative Uncreatedness," where the Taoists meditate on the luminous egg, on the mirror, on primitive androgyny. I should like to make a reference at this point to the way a culture may give greater depth to concepts taken from another very distant culture. For example, for the Greeks and the Romans the poet was the *puer senex,* or aged child, but for the Taoists the name of Lao-tzu meant old-wise-child. We see how in the fifth century B.C., in the period of classical China's great religious upsurge, there appears a more profound concept of the Greco-Roman esteem for the poet.

ARMANDO ALVAREZ BRAVO: Almost an intuition.

JOSÉ LEZAMA LIMA: Quite so. When I was delving deeper into the imaginary eras, studying the great moment of the Etruscans, with their priest king Numa Pompilius, the creator of bronze, of the vestals' cult of fire, and of the king's copulation with the nymph Tacita, I encountered the word *potens,* which, according to Plutarch, represented in priestly Tuscan the "if possible," the infinite possibility we later observe in the *virgo potens* of Catholicism — or, how to engender a god by supernatural means — and I came to the conclusion that it was that infinite possibility that the image must embody. And since the greatest of infinite possibilities is resurrection, poetry — the image — had to express its most encompassing dimension, which is, precisely, resurrection. It was then that I gained the perspective that I set against the Heideggerian theory of man-for-death, proposing a concept of poetry that establishes the prodigious causality of being-for-resurrection, of being that triumphs over death and over the Saturnian realm. So, if you asked me to give a definition of poetry, which would be for me an almost desperate predicament, I would have to do it in these terms: it is the image attained by the man of resurrection. Then I discovered or moved on to another concept: kings as metaphors, and by this I refer to monarchs like Saint Louis, who signed himself *Roi de Tous les Français,* Edward the Confessor, Saint Ferdinand, Saint Elizabeth of Hungary, Alfonso X the Learned, in whom the person came to be constituted in a metaphor that progressed toward a concept of the people as emanating a grace and penetrating into the valley of splendor, into the path of glory, in anticipation of the Day of Resurrection, when everything, even the scars of the saints, will glow with the glow of a stellar metal. This phenomenon appears not only in history but also in particular choral situations. It can be seen in men, in the warriors who sleep in the shadow of the walls they are about to assault. Like those who formed what was called in Napoleon's time the *Grande Armée,* who marched across all Europe. A body of men who in victory or defeat attained to a unity in which the metaphor of their connections took on the totality of an image. In other words, man, a nation, different situations that form certain groupings, may rise to a poetic plenitude. This conception of poetry may even group the animal kingdom into an arrangement of direct poetry with regard to man. A bit more recklessness here, and we can take it a step further. We are on a farm, and suddenly we see what the Oriental masters call the elemental invisible, which turns into a white butterfly. We see how a dark corner is reanimated into a moving shape. It is the spider coming closer to become intoxicated with the music surrounding man. And just as a tree does not walk because it has an aerial perspective, the spider in its web has a wider ambience than man does. A stay at the beach sadly comes to an end. The crab has shared a space with man, and at the end of the season we see it leaving its marks along the highway man takes back to his boredom. We see the frog, in its ancestral position at the mouth of a well, maintaining its statuesque mien as a prince transformed. It shrieks with a trembling of its legs, as if it were about to give birth once more to the prince hidden within its body. Also there are simple human positions that attract a mysterious dialogue in a propitious image, as in some silent sacrifice. A ship plows the waves. A traveler comes to the railing, and his cigarette burns with a slowness that becomes as magnetic as a desert wind. If we close our eyes and then open them, the traveler is no longer alone. By his side, in the night, a shape has been reanimated, similar to that vertebral consciousness that holds together the flight of birds in their autumn migrations. All this is very strange, but. . . . As you can see, there is much to see and try to decipher.

ARMANDO ALVAREZ BRAVO: In the system you have generally outlined, you borrow certain expressions from various authors and historical periods and give them meanings somewhat different from the ones they had in their original contexts. Was that change or expansion necessary in order to integrate them into your system?

JOSÉ LEZAMA LIMA: It was. Knowledge, repeated encounter with those expressions, and meditation helped me enter into the ways of their possibilities. My poetic system unfolds, as is logical to suppose, within the history of culture and of the image, and not within some kind of wild frenzy. Thus, I inscribe at its threshold a series of maxims having very deep resonances. The first is from Saint Paul and says: *caritas omnia credit.* "Charity believes everything." Next to it I place another from Giambattista Vico: the impossible credible. In other words, man, by virtue of being a believer, of dwelling in the world of charity, of believing everything, comes to dwell in a supernatural world filled with gravitational forces. At this point I move on to that vast world extending from Saint Anselm to Nicholas of Cusa, who said in his book *De Docta Ignorantia:* "The greatest things are understood incomprehensibly," meaning that the steps rising up to God, to the Greatest, are understood without comprehension. This can be clarified, on the one hand, by thinking that one can comprehend without understanding. But there is a moment when this comprehension and this understanding come together, and that moment is provided by an acceptance of the *greatest* concept. To close this series, I will allude to a statement by Pascal which clarifies his argument that, since true nature has been lost, everything now can be nature.

The statement is: "It is not good for man not to see anything; neither is it good for him to see so much that he thinks he possesses something; it is good, rather, that he see only enough to be aware of how much he has lost. It is good to see and not to see: this is precisely the state of nature." I have given you four expressions scattered about in these writers' work without implying that they have there the explicit intention I give them in my system. Expressions that in my poetic world are points of reference forming a contrapuntal projection to reach their unity in this new conception of world and image, of enigma and mirror.

ARMANDO ALVAREZ BRAVO: In developing your poetic system, you have indicated, at different times, that with it you aim to arrive at a purely poetic methodology. Would you tell me something about that methodology?

JOSÉ LEZAMA LIMA: I try in my system to destroy Aristotelian causality by seeking a poetic state of unconditionality. But the marvelous thing, which we outlined earlier in relation to metaphor and image, is that this poetic unconditionality has a powerful gravitation, has its bases and its adamantine points of reference. Hence it is possible to speak of poetic ways or of a poetic methodology within that unconditional realm formed by poetry. First, we will cite the Stoics' concept of *occupatio,* that is, of the total occupation of a body. In referring to the image, we have already seen how it covers the substantive ground or resistance of the poem. Next we will cite a concept that seems to us of enormous importance, which we have called "the oblique experience" *[la vivencia oblicua].* This is as if a man, without realizing it, of course, were to create a waterfall in Ontario just by flipping the light switch in his room. We can offer a very obvious example. When Saint George plunges his lance into the dragon, his horse falls down dead.

Observe the following: the mere causal relation would be knight-lance-dragon. The regressive force we could explain by the other causality: dragon-lance-knight; but notice that it is not the knight who falls dead but his horse, according to which the relation is not causal but unconditional. This is the kind of relation we have called "oblique experience." There is also what I have called "the sudden flash" *[el súbito]*, which we can consider as opposite to the Stoic *occupatio*. For example, if a student of German encounters the word *Vogel* (bird), then comes upon the word *Vogelbauer* (birdcage), and then encounters the word *vögeln*, suddenly *[de súbito]*, as the causality bird-birdcage snaps into light like a match, he encounters the unconditional *vögeln*, which gives him the meaning of the bird penetrating into the cage, that is, copulation. There is also what we might call "the hypertelic way or method" *[el camino o método hipertélico]*, in other words, that which always goes beyond its finality by overcoming all determinisms. Another example: for a long time it was believed that a certain kind of ciliary worm would pull back only as far as the tide reached. But it has been observed that even when there is no tide they pull back the same distance. There are animals like the white-headed dipteran that while copulating kill the female. That hypertelic way that always goes beyond its immediate finality, as in this case, is essentially poetic. I see I need again to quote some words, this time from Tertulian, who says, "The son of God was crucified, that is not shameful because it is shameful, and the son of God died, that is all the more credible because it is incredible, and after his burial he returned to life, that is true because it is impossible." From these words we can derive two poetic ways or methods: what is credible because it is incredible (the death of the son of God) and what is true because it is impossible (resurrection). I think I have answered your question.

ARMANDO ALVAREZ BRAVO: You have spoken repeatedly of a return to origins (with regard to poetry, of course), and, in that return, of an elimination of dualism. What can you tell us about that view?

JOSÉ LEZAMA LIMA: Already in my introduction to the first issue of *Orígenes* [in 1944] I tried to stress that. I wanted the poetry appearing in that magazine to be the poetry of a return to magic spells, to rituals, to the living ceremony of primitive man. It's very curious that a poet like Mallarmé, who enjoyed the benefits of a great tradition, should have come in his mature years to long for the magical art of a tribal chieftain, as if that essence of poetry he sought contained both primitivism and the most extreme refinement. Similarly, we can stress that in his "Prose pour des Esseintes" he speaks of the *hyperbole de ma mémoire,* a position very close to that of Descartes, when, as part of the methodical doubt of his intellectualist philosophy, he mentions what he calls hyperbolic doubt, repeating the famous argument that excessive doubt, the radical *dubito,* culminates in total, hyperbolic affirmation. Thus, what was involved for us was a problem concerning the incarnation of poetry, or, to put it in a language recalling that of theology, the hypostasis of poetry. What was involved was finding a foothold for poetry, an incarnation of metaphor and of image in historical temporality. Thus, metaphor was as much a matter of metamorphosis as it was of *metanoia,* or — what amounts to the same thing — of successive transmutations of body and soul, offering all the suggestiveness and fascination of metaphor as a *metanoia* that goes beyond simple metamorphosis to produce a transmutation of the animus. Since I've now spoken of metaphor, I'll make another reference to image. I should like what I mean in this dimension to be clearly seen. If we proceed on the basis of Pascal's claim that since true nature has been lost, all can be nature, we can situate the image in a precise area of striking fascination. In the first place, image is a substituted nature. In the second, image covers the frightful destiny of the house of Atreus, for only it can clarify for us that frightful destiny. It clarifies for us the poetic concept of the entire ancient world.

ARMANDO ALVAREZ BRAVO: And what about the modern world?

JOSÉ LEZAMA LIMA: I think that in the case of Baudelaire, there is a return to *arete* or poetry as destiny, as sacrifice, and to *aristeia,* or Pallas's protection of Diomedes as it appears in book 6 of the *Iliad.* You can see, therefore, why that image has to appear obscure. It *is* obscure, torn from the very darkness of night. But that darkness or obscurity seems to repeat Oedipus's memorable words: "Ah, darkness, my light." Of course, both that *arete* and that *aristeia* must entail an asceticism resulting from the prodigious accumulations bestowed by the joy of a lineage of the best. So the poet, by means of the image, makes himself master of nature and offers the most seductive of asceticisms, the only kind that can be tolerated, just as the basket makers of New Guinea were born with their umbilical cords wrapped around their necks or the kings of Georgia were born with the marks of their royal nature inscribed upon their left nipples.

ARMANDO ALVAREZ BRAVO: Do you have any thesis regarding words used in a poetic sense?

JOSÉ LEZAMA LIMA: Already in ancient times, Pythagoras cast a great deal of light on the different varieties of the word. There are simple words, hieroglyphic words, and symbolic words. That is, words that express, words that conceal, and words that signify. When today, guided by the latest discoveries of German philology, we speak of the meaning of poetry, we realize that already Pythagoras had told us about words that signify, about symbolic words.

ARMANDO ALVAREZ BRAVO: Of those varieties postulated by the philosopher, which have you preferred?

JOSÉ LEZAMA LIMA: The poet makes use of all of Pythagoras's words or varieties, but he also goes beyond them. He manages to express a kind of *supra verba,* which is actually the word in all its three dimensions of expressivity, concealment, and sign. I would say there is a fourth kind of word, which is the only one for poetry. A word to which I will not give a name, but which, based on the progressions of image and metaphor and on the resistance of the image, strengthens the body of poetry. I want you to keep in mind that all these things we've been talking about take place in the realm of what the harmonious Greeks called *terateia,* marvel, portent. You will recall that the whole atmosphere of *Prometheus* — of Aeschylus's *Prometheus* — takes place in the *terateia.* Aristotle clarifies this concept when he says that Aeschylus set about to achieve more of a marvelous surprise than an illusion of reality.

ARMANDO ALVAREZ BRAVO: In that statement Aristotle posits two esthetic positions. Which do you believe is decisive?

JOSÉ LEZAMA LIMA: I believe that contemporary man has attained to a position that surpasses that of the world of the Greeks. Scientific research concerning the structure of reality testifies to its symmetry and beauty. If we contemplate the staggered layers of sand left by a simoom, forming a kind of enormous coliseum, what we see combines marvel and surprise with a realistic illusion deriving from the laws of optics and our modern concept of perspective. But I'm going to pick up again the thread of what I was saying before, which I think will offer some clarification concerning your question. The Catholic lives in the supernatural realm and lends greater depth to the Greek concept of *terateia,* for he is imbued with the Pauline effort to give substance to faith, to find a substance for what cannot be seen, what cannot be heard, what cannot be touched, attaining, in poetry, to a world of full, valid signification.

ARMANDO ALVAREZ BRAVO: And what about the non-Catholic, the atheist? What signification will he find? Where will it come from?

JOSÉ LEZAMA LIMA: Well, can you imagine the case of a man who writes poetry and doesn't believe in anything at all?

ARMANDO ALVAREZ BRAVO: I think all men believe in something. Since we are talking about poetry, what I would specifically like to know is how your poetic system accounts for the poetry written by a man who does not proceed on the basis of any religious conception. A man who is not a Catholic.

JOSÉ LEZAMA LIMA: Look, Robespierre himself spoke of the Goddess Reason, just as Lucretius, the atomistic genius of atheism, talked about whirlwinds and furies and other forces of nature and considered them gods. Aside from the fact that a man cannot deny the great contributions of the Orient, of the Greco-Roman world, of the sum of all that anteriority that Catholicism assimilated with exemplary reason and intuition, in accordance with the Pauline maxim that reveals the meaning of being indebted: "To Greeks and Romans, ancients and moderns, to all I am indebted." Though an atheistic poet may deny all these contributions, he cannot fail to turn within their ambience. I'll remind you of a contemporary example. We all know that Valéry always professed his atheism. But when he gave his definition of poetry, he called it "the paradise of language." You see how this atheist uses the word "paradise" with all the resonance of a Catholic. Besides, we have his studies of Leonardo, in which he praises the position derived from the Council of Trent about the soul and the body being intertwined, forming a unity, and about there being a mystery of the body and a mystery of the soul that in man are ready for his transfiguration. With this concept of transfiguration, the Catholic world surpassed the Greek concept of metamorphosis, in which the memory of the previous stage is obliterated by sleep.

ARMANDO ALVAREZ BRAVO: This is Valéry's conception. But for many people, and I'm sorry to keep insisting, there is no soul, and yet that attitude does not prevent them from writing poetry. How do you reconcile these facts?

JOSÉ LEZAMA LIMA: My friend, I've always believed my poetic system is something beautiful in itself, but I've never been so arrogant as to believe it is something unique. Above it I place poetry, poetry as the most transparent of mysteries, or, if you wish, as mysterious transparency. That ambiguity allows me to say to you that it is not I but rather time that must answer that question: time that makes poetry and poetry that makes in time. We both serve poetry and all those who do the same will agree with me when I say that in the end poetry will unify everything; it is already beginning to do so. I don't think there's anything else to say.

ARMANDO ALVAREZ BRAVO: Or everything's left to be said.

JOSÉ LEZAMA LIMA: Or both.

• JI •

TO REACH LEZAMA LIMA (1967)

JULIO CORTÁZAR

Después que en las arenas, sedosas pausas intermedias, entre lo
irreal sugerido y el denso, irrechazable aparecido, se hizo el acuario
métrico, y el ombligo terrenal superó el vicioso horizonte que con-
fundía al hombre con la reproducción de los árboles.

José Lezama Lima, *Para llegar a la Montego Bay*

"Est-ce que ce monsieur est fou?" me dit-elle.
Je fis un signe affirmatif.
"Et il vous emmène avec lui?"
Même affirmation.
"Ou çela?" dit-elle.
J'indique du doigt le centre de la terre.

Jules Verne, *Voyage au centre de la terre*

These pages on José Lezama Lima's novel *Paradiso* (Ediciones Union,
1966) are not intended as a study of Lezama's novelistic technique,
which would require a rigorous analysis of all his work as a poet and
an essayist, informed by the most significant developments in the field
of anthropology (Bachelard, Eliade, Gilbert Durand . . .); rather, they

represent the sympathetic approach that Cronopios employ to establish commerce with each other. Why Lezama Lima? Because, as he says describing one of his characters:

"What I like about him," Cemí answered, "is his way of putting himself at the umbilical center of issues. It gives me the impression that during every moment of his growth he was endowed with grace. He has what the Chinese call *li,* that is, behavior of a cosmic orientation, configuration, the perfect form that comes before a fact, perhaps what our classical tradition might call beauty within a style. Like a strategist who always offers a flank well guarded against attack, he can't be surprised. As he advances, he seems to keep an eye on the rear echelon. He knows what he lacks and looks for it avidly. He has a maturity that doesn't become enslaved as he grows and a wisdom that doesn't reject the immediate happening but at the same time doesn't render it a worshipful idolatry. His wisdom has excellent luck. He's a student who always knows what question he's going to be asked; but fate, of course, acts in a continuum where the answer leaps forth like a spark. He begins by studying the hundred questions in such a way that he can't miss, and the question that the bird of fortune brings in its beak is precisely the fruit he likes, which is the best one and the one the most worth the trouble of polishing and inspection." (279–80)*

So are we both crazy? Where can I emerge, desperate for air, from this deep swim through the hundreds of pages of *Paradiso?* And why does Jules Verne pop up all of a sudden in a discussion of a book where nothing seems to evoke him? And yet, yes, certainly it evokes him, doesn't Lezama speak of parallel existences, hasn't he somewhere said that it is "as if, without realizing it, by switching on the lights in his

---

*Quotations from *Paradiso* for which page references are given are translated by Gregory Rabassa and refer to the edition published by Farrar, Straus and Giroux, 1974.

room a man initiated a waterfall in Ontario" — a Vernian metaphor if ever there was one. Don't we place ourselves in that tangential causality when we remember that the moment Saint George stuck his lance into the dragon the first to fall dead was his horse, just as lightning will sometimes pass down the trunk of an oak and run inoffensively through thirteen seminarians absorbed in eating Gruyère and hunting for four-leaf clovers, before carbonizing a canary stridulating in a cage fifty yards away? So, yes, Jules Verne, so to reach Montego Bay you surely must pass through the center of the earth. It is not only certain but it is literal, and here is the proof: very rare reader of *Paradiso* (I imagine, in my vanity, a very exclusive club of those who, like you, have read *The Man Without Qualities, The Death of Virgil,* and *Paradiso;* in this alone — I am referring to the club — I resemble Phileas Fogg), do you realize that the explicit reference to Verne diabolically appears in an episode of eroticism like the one some researchers are cautiously beginning to attribute to the father of the *Nautilus?* In this episode the priapic oarsman Leregas will receive a visit from the unsuspected athlete Baena Albornoz. Baena descends to the underworld of a Havana gymnasium where, like a consenting Adonis, he is penetrated by the boar's tusk that makes him bite the bed in an ecstasy of delight. During Leregas's tense wait for the humiliating visit of the Hercules who, after many diurnal labors, spins the feminine thread of his true condition in the night, "the memory of the crater of Iasshole went down to the basement, the shadows of Scataris also reached there. The ringed shadow of Scataris over the crater of Sneffels . . ." (243). Fiendishly, the innocent island orography resonates through a lasciviously erotic situation, and Arne Saknussemm, marvel of our youth (*Descends dans la cratère du Yocul de Sneffels que l'ombre du Scartars vient caresser avant les calendes de Juillet, voyageur audacieux, et tu parviendras au centre de la Terre . . .*) proposes through sounds and images a lubricious revelation. Iasshole ("Yoculo"), ringed shadow ("il a perdu ses trente deux plis," a character of Jean Genet's would say, referring to another Baena Albornoz), Sneffels, who makes you think of "to sniff," Scataris, who in this context evokes the scrotum, and the images of descent into the crater, of caresses, of shadowy regions . . . O Phileas Fogg, O Professor Lidenbrock, what are we doing to your father?

I will let the recluse of Nantes and his speleologists lie in peace, but first I want to consider another passage so significant that Lezama could have placed it, like a blazing light, at the head of all that follows:

> Enfin, mon oncle me tirant par le collet, j'arrivai près de la boule.
> "Regarde, me dit-il, et regarde bien! il faut prendre des *leçons* d'abîme." (Jules Verne, *Voyage au centre de la terre*)

In ten days, stopping only to breathe and feed my cat, Theodor W. Adorno, I read *Paradiso,* completing (completing?) a journey begun several years before with the reading of some of its chapters in the review *Orígenes,* along with other objects of Tlon or Ugbar. I am not a critic; someday, far in the future most likely, this prodigious oeuvre will find its Maurice Blanchot, because it will take someone like that to forge the way. I intend only to point out the shameful ignorance of this work and to strike a blow in advance against the misunderstandings that will arise when Latin America finally hears the voice of the author of *Paradiso.* The ignorance does not surprise me; twelve years ago I did not know of Lezama Lima either, until Ricardo Vigon, in Paris, told me about *Oppiano Licario,* which had just been published in *Orígenes,* and which now closes (if anything can) *Paradiso.* I doubt that in these dozen years the work of Lezama has reached anywhere near the audience that has greeted the work of Jorge Luis Borges or Octavio Paz, after an equal time, even though Lezama's work is undeniably on their level. Difficulties of matter and manner are the first causes of that ignorance: reading Lezama is one of the most arduous and at times frustrating tasks that one can undertake. The perseverance demanded by writers who work the limits, such as Raymond Roussel, Hermann Broch, or the Cuban master, is rare even among "specialists": thus the vacant chairs in our club. Borges and Paz (I chose them to set our sights on our countries' crowning achievements) have the advantage over Lezama of being writers of midday light, I would almost call them Apollonian in the sense that they possess perfectly composed styles and coherent organization of thought. Their difficulties and even obscurities (Apollo also knew how to be nocturnal, to descend into the abyss to kill the serpent Python) respond to a dialectic evoked by *Le Cimetière marin:*

> . . . Mais rendre la lumière
> Suppose d'ombre une morne moitié.

Endpoints of a tradition of Mediterranean origin, Borges and Paz produce their best effects without first posing the three riddles that turn the reader of Lezama into an eternal Oedipus. And if I say that this is an advantage they have over Lezama, I refer to those readers who have an almost moral abhorrence for the trials of Oedipus, who seek the greatest yield with the least effort. In Argentina, at least, there is a tendency to shy away from hermeticism, and Lezama is not only hermetic in the literal sense that the best of his work supposes an apprehension of essences through the mythical and the esoteric in all their historic, psychic, and literary forms, combined in an absolutely vertiginous manner within a poetic system where a Louis XV chair will often serve to seat the god Anubis; but he is also hermetic in the formal sense, as much by an innocence that leads him to believe that the most irregular of his metaphoric systems will be understood perfectly as by his original baroque style (one that is baroque *in origin,* as opposed to a baroque lucidly *mis en page,* as Alejo Carpentier's). You can see how difficult it is to join this club when so many obstacles stand in your way, except that the pleasures begin with these very difficulties, which make me, for one, read Lezama in the spirit of someone trying to decode the cipher *messunkaSebrAlicefdok, segnittamurtn,* etc., which finally is resolved into *Descends dans le cratère du Yocul de Sneffels* . . . : one might say that haste and the sense of guilt caused by bibliographic proliferation have led the modern reader to reject, at times with condescension, all *trobar clus.* Add false asceticism and the solemn blinders of wrongheaded specialization, against which a spirit represented by structuralism is now arising. In a work of masterful unitive intuition Goethe melded philosophy and poetry, previously separate in his century; until Thomas Mann (I am speaking now of the novel) it seemed that authors and readers would retain that synthesis, but already in Robert Musil (to stay in the German literary tradition) this sort of achievement no longer met the acclaim it deserved. Today the reader tends to adopt the specialist's attitude as he reads, often unconsciously rejecting works that offer mixed waters, novels that enter the realm of poetry, or metaphysics applied to an elbow on the bar counter or a bedpillow used for amorous activities. He is fairly tolerant of the extraliterary cargo any novel carries, as long as the genre observes its basic assumptions (which, I might add in passing, nobody understands very well, but that is another question). *Paradiso,* a novel that is also a hermetic tract, a poetics and the poetry that results from it, will have trouble reading its readers: Where does the novel begin and the poetry end? What is the meaning of this anthropology embedded in an augury that is at the same time a tropical folklore that is also a family chronicle? One hears much these days of "diagonal" (interdisciplinary) sciences, but the *diagonal reader* is slow to appear, and *Paradiso,* that transverse slice of essences and presences, will encounter the resistance that greets anything opposed to the direct file of received ideas. Yet the slice has been made; as in the Chinese story of the perfect executioner, the decapitated one will remain standing, not realizing that the first sneeze will send his head rolling across the ground.

If the difficulties of his expression are the first reason why Lezama is not well-known, our political and historical circumstances are the second. Since 1960, fear, hypocrisy, and guilty consciences have combined to separate Cuba, its intellectuals, and its artists, from the rest of Latin America. Known writers such as Guillen, Carpentier, and Wilfredo Lam have surmounted this barrier by means of international reputations acquired before the revolution, so they cannot be ignored. Lezama, at that time still inexcusably near the bottom of the hierarchy of values drawn up by Peruvian, Mexican, or Argentine scholars, has remained on the other side of the barrier, so that those who have heard of him and want to read *Tratados en la Habana, Analecta del reloj, La fijeza, La expresión americana,* or *Paradiso* cannot find copies. Like many other Cuban poets and artists, he has been forced to live and work in an isolation of which we can say only that it is sickening and shameful. Of course we must close the door to totalitarian communism. *Paradiso?* Nothing that could justify that label could emerge from its inferno. Rest assured, the OAS is watching over you.

There is also, perhaps, a third, and more hidden, reason for the oppressive silence that surrounds Lezama's work: I am going to speak of it without mincing words precisely because the few Cuban critics familiar with his work have chosen not to mention it, but I know its negative effect in the hands of many Pharisees of Latin American letters. I am referring to the numerous formal errors in Lezama Lima's prose, which, in contrast to the subtlety and profundity of its content, produce a scandalized impatience that the superficially refined reader can rarely get beyond. Lezama's publisher does a very poor job on the typographic level and *Paradiso* is no exception, so when the novel's internal perplexities are compounded by the carelessness that produces orthographic and grammatical extravagances, the eyes of the stuffed shirt within us have to roll. Several years ago when I began to show or read passages of Lezama to people who didn't know his work, the astonishment caused by his vision of reality and the audacious images that communicate it was nearly always tainted by an ironic smile of superiority. I soon realized that a defense mechanism entered into play and that, threatened with the absolute, people quickly exaggerated the importance of his formal faults as an almost unconscious pretext for remaining on this side of Lezama, rather than following him as he boldly plunges into deep waters. The undeniable fact that Lezama seems to have decided never to write correctly any English, French, or Russian name, and that his quotations from foreign languages are replete with orthographic fantasies, induces the typical Rio de la Plata intellectual to see him as a no less typical autodidact of an underdeveloped country, which is quite accurate, and to find in this a justification for not appreciating his true significance, which is most unfortunate. Of course, among particular Argentines, formal correctness in writing as well as in dress is a guarantee of seriousness, and anyone who announces that the earth is round in the proper "style" deserves more respect than a Cronopio with a spud in his mouth but plenty to say behind it. I speak of Argentina because I know it a little, but when I was in Cuba there too I met young intellectuals who smiled condescendingly in recalling the peculiar way Lezama pronounced the name of some foreign poet; the difference came out when we began to discuss the poet in question: while these young people never got beyond good phonetics, in five minutes Lezama had them staring at their hands, at a loss for words. One of the indices of underdevelopment is our fastidiousness toward anything that peels away the cultural crust, appearances, the lock on the door of culture. We know that Dylan is pronounced *Dilan,* not *Dailan,* the way we said it ourselves for the first time (and they looked at us ironically or corrected us or made us feel we had done something wrong); we know exactly how to pronounce Caen or Laon and Sean O'Casey and Gloucester. And that's fine, like keeping your underarms clean and using deodorant. What is really important comes later, or not at all. For many of those who dismiss Lezama with a smile, it will arrive neither sooner nor later, and yet their armpits, I assure you, are perfect.

The remarkable ingenuity of Lezama's narrative has the same effect on many readers as its surface flaws do. Yet it is because of my love for that ingenuity that I am speaking about him here — not bound by any scholastic canon, it possesses an extraordinary efficacy: while many search, Perceval meets; while many talk, Mishkin comprehends. The baroque that arises from many sources in Latin America has produced writers as different and yet as alike as Vallejo, Neruda, Asturias, and Carpentier (I am speaking of substance rather than genre), but in Lezama's case it is distinguished by a quality that I can only call, for want of a better word, ingenuity. An American ingenuity, insular in both a literal and a broader sense, an American innocence. An ingenious American innocence, opening its eyes eleatically, orphically, at the very beginning of Creation. Lezama Adam before the fall, Lezama Noah identical to the one in the Flemish paintings who sagely directs the file of animals: two butterflies, two horses, two leopards, two ants, two dolphins. . . . A primitive, as everyone knows, an accomplished *sorbonnard,* but American the way the dissected albatross of the prophet of Ecclesiastes did not become a "sadder but wiser man," even though his science was metempsychosis: his knowledge is original, jubilant, it is born of the water of Tales and the fire of Empedocles. Between the thought of Lezama and that of a European writer (or his Rio Platan homologues, much less American in respect to the matter under discussion), we find the difference between innocence and guilt. All European writers are "slaves of their baptism," if I may paraphrase Rimbaud; like it or not, their writing carries baggage from an immense and almost frightening tradition; they accept that tradition or they fight against it, it inhabits them, it is their familiar and their succubus. Why write, if everything has, in a way, already been said? Gide observed sardonically that since nobody listened, everything has to be said again, yet a suspicion of guilt and superfluity leads the European intellectual to the most extreme refinement of his trade and tools, the only way to avoid paths too much traveled. Thus the enthusiasm that greets novelties, the uproar when a writer has succeeded in giving substance to a new slice of the invisible; merely recall symbolism, surrealism, the "nouveau roman": finally something truly new that neither Ronsard, nor Stendhal, nor Proust imagined. For a moment we can put aside our guilt; even the epigones begin to believe they are doing something new. Afterward, slowly, they start to feel European again and each writer still has his albatross around his neck.

While this is going on, Lezama wakes up on his island with a preadamite happiness, without a fig leaf, innocent of any direct tradition. He assumes them all, from the Etruscan interpreting entrails to Leopold Bloom blowing his nose in a dirty handkerchief, but without historic compromise, without being a French or an Austrian writer; he is Cuban with only a handful of his own culture behind him and the rest is knowledge, pure and free, not a career responsibility. He can write whatever he pleases without saying now Rabelais . . . now

Martial . . . He is not a chained slave, he is not required to write more, or better, or differently, he doesn't have to justify himself as a writer. His incredible gifts, like his deficiencies, spring out of this innocent freedom, this free innocence. At times, reading *Paradiso,* one has the feeling that Lezama has come from another planet; how is it possible to ignore or defy the taboos of knowledge to this extent, the *don't-write-like-this*es that are our embarrassing professional mandates? When the innocent American makes his appearance, the good savage who accumulates trinkets without suspecting that they are worthless or out of fashion, then two things can happen to Lezama. One, the one that counts: the eruption, with the primordial force of the stealer of fire, of a brilliance stripped of the inferiority complexes that weigh so heavily on Latin Americans. The other, which makes the impeccably cultured reader smile ironically, is the Douanier Rousseau route, the route of Mishkin simplicity, the person who puts a period at the end of an extraordinary passage in *Paradiso* and writes with the utmost tranquility: "What happened to young Ricardo Fronesis, while the story of his ancestors was being told?"

I am writing these pages because I *know* that sentences like the one I have just quoted count more with the pedants than the prodigious inventiveness with which *Paradiso* creates its world. And if I quote the sentence about young Fronesis it is because, like many other gaucheries, it annoys me too, but only the way I would be annoyed by a fly on a Picasso or a scratch from my cat Theodor while I am listening to the music of Xenakis. Anyone who finds himself incapable of grasping the complexities of a work hides his withdrawal behind the most superficial pretexts because he had not gotten past the surface. Thus, I knew a gentleman who refused to listen to classical records because, he said, the sound of the needle on the plastic prevented him from enjoying the work in its absolute perfection; motivated by this lofty standard, he spent days listening to tangos and boleros that would curl your hair. Whenever I quote a passage from Lezama and am met by an ironic smile or a change of subject, I think of that man; those who are incapable of penetrating *Paradiso* always react that way: for them everything is the scritch of the needle, a fly, a scratch. In *Hopscotch* I defined and attacked the Lady Reader who is incapable of waging true amorous battle against the book, a battle like that of Job with the angel. For those who question the legitimacy of my attack, one example will suffice: at first the respected critics of Buenos Aires could not understand the two possible ways of reading my book; after that they went on to the *pollice verso* with the pathetic assurance that they had read the book "in the two ways demanded by the author," when what the poor author had offered was an option: I never had the vanity to believe that in our time people were going to read a book twice. What then would you expect from the Lady Reader faced with *Paradiso,* which, as one of Lewis Carroll's characters said, would try the patience of an oyster? But there is no patience where we have lost humility and hope, where a conditioned, prefabricated culture, adulated by those writers we can call functional, with its rebellions and heterodoxies carefully controlled by the marquises of Queensbury of the profession, rejects all works that go truly against the grain. Willing to confront any literary difficulty on the intellectual or psychological plane as long as the Western rules of the game are observed, ready to play the most arduous Proustian or Joycean chess game as long as it employs known pieces and divinable strategies, she retreats indignant and ironic when she is invited into an extrageneric territory, to react to language and action that are part of a narrative that is born not of books but of long *readings of the abyss;* and I have now finished my explanation of my epigraph and it is time to pass to another subject.

Is *Paradiso* a novel? Yes, inasmuch as it is tied loosely together by the life of José Cemí — from which the multiple episodes and connected and unconnected stories arise and to which they return. But right from the beginning this "argument" has curious characteristics. I don't know if Lezama realizes that the beginning of his book recalls the delights of *Tristram Shandy,* for while José Cemí is indeed alive at the beginning of the book, whereas Tristram, who tells his own story, is not born until the middle of the book, still the protagonist around whom *Paradiso* revolves remains in the background while the book proceeds leisurely to describe the lives of his grandparents, parents, aunts, and uncles. More importantly, *Paradiso* lacks what I would call the unifying reverse-field, the fabric that makes a novel, however fragmentary its episodes. This is not a defect, for the book does not at all depend on its being or not being what we expect from a novel; my own reading of *Paradiso,* as of all of Lezama, begins by expecting the unexpected, by not demanding a novel, and then I can concentrate on its content without useless tension, without that petulant protest that arises from opening a cabinet to get out the jam and discovering instead three fantastic vests. Lezama has to be read with a suspension prior to the *fatum,* just as one gets into a plane without asking the color of the pilot's eyes or his religious beliefs. What irritates the critical intelligence in the Bureau of Weights and Measures seems perfectly natural to any critical intelligence thrust into the cave of Ali Baba.

Paradiso may not be a novel, because of its lack of a plot capable of providing narrative coherence to the dizzying multiplicity of its contents, as much as anything. Toward the end, for example, Lezama interjects a chapter-long story that seems to have nothing to do with the rest of the novel, although its atmosphere and impact are the same. And the two final chapters are dominated by Oppiano Licario, who had hardly appeared previously, while José Cemí has all but disappeared, along with Fronesis and Foción; consequently, these chapters have something of the nature of appendixes, of *surplus*. But more than its unconventional structure it is its lack of a viable (that is, "life-like") spatio-temporal and psychological reference that is not novelistic. All of the characters are seen more in essence than in presence; they are archetypes more than types. The first result of this (which has raised some eyebrows) is that, while the novel tells its story of several Cuban families at the end of the past century and the beginning of this one, with profuse historical detailing of geography, furniture, gastronomy, and fashion, the characters themselves seem to move in a perfect continuum outside historicity, talking to each other in a private, unchanging language that does not pertain either to the reader or the story and has no reference to psychological or cultural verisimilitude.

And yet, nothing is less inconceivable than this language when one is freed from the persistent notion of the realism of the novel, which is primary even in the novel's fantastic or poetic forms. Nothing is more *natural* than a language that emerges from native roots and origins, that always lies between oracle and incantation, that is the shadow of myths, the murmur of the collective unconscious; nothing is more human, finally, than such a poetic language, disdainful of prosaic and pragmatic information, a verbal radiaesthesia that divines the deepest waters and makes them gush forth. No one who understands he is reading an epic is put off by the language of the *Iliad* or the Norse sagas; the speeches of the Greek chorus are barely noticed in the amplitude of the tragedy (and this applies to a Paul Claudel or a Christopher Fry as well). Why then not accept the fact that the characters of *Paradiso* always speak *desde la imagen,* that they are presented through a poetic system that Lezama has often described, whose key is the power of the image as the supreme expression of the human spirit in search of the reality of the invisible world?

Thus, when two Cuban boys form a friendship at school, they speak like this:

> "From the first day of class," Fibo told José Eugenio, "I could see that you were the son of a Spaniard. You never did anything bad; you never looked surprised; you never seemed to notice other people doing bad things. Still, after we settled into our desks, a person's eyes would light on you. You've got a bottom like a root. When you're standing up you look as if you're growing, but inwardly, toward a dream. Nobody ever notices that kind of growth."
>
> "When I went into that classroom," José Eugenio replied, "I was so disturbed that it clouded over, it seemed to be raining. I was touching mist, I was pinching the ink of a squid. So your jabbing point made me realize where I was, it straightened me out, it touched me and I wasn't a tree any more." (87)

And a dialogue like this occurs during a family meal:

> The chill of November, cut by gusts of north wind which rustled the tops of the Prado poplars, justified the arrival of the glistening turkey, its harsh extremities softened by butter, its breast capable of attracting the appetite of the whole family and sheltering it as in an ark of the covenant.
>
> "The Mexican turkey buzzard is much tenderer," the older Santurce child said.
>
> "Not turkey buzzard, just turkey," Cemí corrected. "Once for my asthma they recommended a soup made from the young of that disgusting bird, if I can avoid using its ugly name, but I said I'd rather die than drink that oil. That kind of soup must taste like the sow's milk that the ancients thought caused leprosy."

"We really don't know what that disease comes from," Dr. Santurce said. As a doctor, he did not feel it improper to talk about illnesses at dinnertime.

"Let's talk about the Peking nightingale instead," Doña Augusta said, annoyed at the turn of the conversation. Cemí's reference to sow's milk had been comical because it was so unexpected, but Santurce's development of the theme at that moment was as frightening as the possibilities of a tidal wave that the evening papers had begun to brood over.

"The red stains on the tablecloth must have favored the Vulturidae theme, but remember too, Mother, that the Peking nightingale sang for a dying emperor," Alberto said as he started to parcel out the winy, almondy turkey.

"I know, Alberto, that every meal must pass through its gloomy whirlwind, because a happy family gathering couldn't get by without death trying to open the windows, but the aroma of that turkey can be a spell to drive away Hera the horrible." (182–83)

Doña Augusta invokes Hera, any servant recalls Hermes, Nero, or Yi King. Lezama makes absolutely no effort to make his characters' speech appropriate to their conditions, to have them vary their speech in different situations or when speaking to different people; yet this is the magic of the novel, for as one's reading advances the characters differentiate and define themselves, Ricardo Fronesis reveals his most secret depths, Foción is set against him like an antistrophe, the way *yin* calls forth *yang,* José Cemí and Alberta Olalla, Oppiano Licario and Doña Augusta, José Eugenio and Rialta, each of these is a person, just as Andromache and Philoctetes and Creon are in the realm of tragedy. Lezama accomplishes the non-Goethean feat of creating the individual out of the universal, almost disdainfully rejecting the novelist's usual strategies of typification for character and exaggeration for portraiture. Because characters aren't important to Lezama, the important thing is the total mystery of human experience, "the existence of a universal marrow which controls series and exceptions" (p. 328). Thus the author's favored characters live, act, think, and talk in conformity to a total poetics that appears in the following passages, several more doors through which we can enter the verbal universe of *Paradiso:*

> But neither the historical nor futurity nor tradition awaken man's exercise or conduct, and he's been the one who has seen it most clearly and deeply. But the desire, the desire that becomes choral, the desire that, when it penetrates, succeeds, by the surface of the shared dream, in elaborating the true warp of the historical, that escaped him. *Difficult it is to fight against desire; what it wants it buys with the soul:* Heraclitus' aphorism encompasses the totality of man's conduct. The only thing attained by the suprahistoric is desire, which doesn't end in dialogue but reflects on the universal spirit, prior to the actual appearance of the earth.
>
> We may discuss Nietzsche's will to transvaluate all values, but the values that must be found and established are very different now than the ones he considered. A gathering of scholars who approach new assignments in the future, for example: the history of fire, of the drop of water, of the breath, of the emanation of Greek *aporrhoea.* A history of fire, beginning with a presentation of its fight with the Neptunic or aqueous elements, the dissemination of fire, fire in the tree, colors of the flame, the blaze and the wind, the burning bush of Moses, the sun and the white rooster, the sun and the red rooster among the Germani, in short, the transformations of fire into energy, all those themes which are the first that occur to me and which today's man needs to enter new regions of depth. (305)

On Foción's homosexual love for Fronesis:

> The error that Foción's senses brought as he neared Fronesis consisted in that the image was the form which for him acquired the insatiable. But just as he intuited that he would never be able to sate himself with Fronesis's body (for a long time he had been convinced

that, without even proposing it to him, Fronesis was playing with him, gaining a perspective where in the end he was grotesquely knocked off his horse), he had made a transposition in which his verbum of sexual energy no longer solicited the other body, that is, no longer sought its incarnation, going from the fact to the body, but, on the contrary, starting out from his body he attained the aeration, the subtilizing, the absolute pneuma of the other body. He volatilized the figure of Fronesis, but there was his insatiability, reconstructing the fragments to attain even the possibility of his image, where his senses again felt shaken by an unsupported fervor, one could say a falcon in pursuit of a pneuma, the very spirit of flight. (326)

The worldview of Fronesis, Cemí, and Foción:

When the rest of the students appeared disdainful and mocking and the majority of professors were unable to overcome their aphasias and lethargyrations, Fronesis, Cemí, and Foción scandalized people by bringing the new gods, the word without breaking, in its pure yolk yellow, and the combinatorials and the proportions that could trace new games and new ironies. They knew that conformity in expression and in ideas took on in the contemporary world innumerable variants and disguises, because it exacted from the intellectual a servitude, the mechanism of a causative absolute, so that he would abandon his truly heroic position of being, as in the grand epochs, creator of values, of forms, the salutatorian of creative vitalism and the accuser of what is enshrouded in blocks of ice, which still dares to float in the river of the temporal. (329)

José Cemí conversing with his grandmother:

"Grandmother, every day I am more aware of how Mama is coming to look like you. Both of you have what I would call the same interpreted rhythm of nature. Lately, people have a trapped look, as if they had no way out. But you two seem guided, as if you were giving effect to the words that made their way into your ears. All you have to do is listen, follow a sound . . . You are free from interruptions, when you talk you don't seem to look for words but rather to follow a point that will make everything clear. It's as if you were acting in obedience, as if you'd sworn to keep the quantity of light in the world from diminishing. We know that both of you have made a sacrifice, that you've renounced vast regions, life itself, I would say, if something had not appeared within you, a life so miraculous that the rest of us don't even know what we exist for, or how to live out our days, because it seems that we are mere fragments of the upper sphere that the mystics talk of, and have not yet found the island where stags and senses leap."

"But, my dear grandson Cemí, you observe all this in your mother and myself precisely because your gift is to grasp that rhythm of growth for nature. An infrequent lingering, that lingering of nature, before which you place an observant lingering which is itself nature. Thank God that the lingering in bringing observation to a fabulous dimension is accompanied by a hyperbolic memory. Among many gestures, many words, many sounds, after you've observed them between sleep and waking, you know the one that will accompany your memory over the centuries. The visit of our impressions possesses an intangible swiftness, but your gift of observation lies in wait, as if in a theater through which must pass again and again those impressions that later become as light as larvae, that allow themselves to be caressed or show their disdain; afterwards memory gives them a substance like primal mud, like a stone that collects the image of the fish's shadow. You talk about the rhythm of growth in nature, but one must have much humility to observe it, follow it, revere it. In that, too, it's apparent you belong to our family, most people interrupt, prefer the void, make exclamations, stupid demands, or deliver phantom arias, but you pay attention to the rhythm that makes a complement, the complement of the unknown, but which, as you say, has been dictated to us as the principal mark of our lives. We've been dictated to, that is, we were necessary for the complement of a higher voice to touch the shore, feel itself on solid ground. The rhythmic interpretation of the higher voice, almost without the intervention of the will, that is, a will already wrapped in a superior destiny, gave us the enjoyment of an impulse which was simultaneously a clarification . . ." (370–71)

Although Lezama's synthesis is not easy to convey, this passage may give an idea of the occult rhythms that animate his narrative:

The exercise of poetry, the verbal search for unknown finality, developed in him a strange perspicacity for words which acquire an animistic relief when grouped in space, seated like sibyls at an assembly of spirits. When his vision gave him a word in whatever relation it might have to reality, that word seemed to pass into his hands, and although the word remained invisible, freed of the vision from whence it had come, it went along, gathering a wheel on which gyrated incessantly its invisible modulation and its palpable modelization; then between intangible modelization and almost visible modulation, he seemed finally to be able to touch its forms, if he closed his eyes a little. Thus he went on acquiring the ambivalence between gnostic space, which expresses, which knows, which has a difference of density that contracts to bring forth, and quantity, which in the unity of time revives the look, the sacred character of what in one instant passes from undulant vision into fixed look. Gnostic space, tree, man, city, spatial groupages in which man is the median point between nature and the supernatural. (355–56)

Meditating on that, José Cemí approaches an antiquarian's window, where a group of statuettes and other objects seem to suffer from a lack of harmony, from the reciprocal relation of their forces, which vainly seek coincidence, articulations, fraternal rhythms. Cemí understands that every time he chooses and buys an object, his choice is due to "his glance having distinguished and isolated it from the rest of the objects, moving it forward like a chess piece that penetrates a world that instantaneously reconstitutes all its facets," an intuitive process that the reader of *Paradiso* perceives in every episode, every decisive crossroads within the story. Cemí knows that "the piece advanced represented a point that synthesized an infinite current of relations": there could not be a better description of the process that, like Valéry's *Achille immobile à grand pas,* at once sets in tumultuous movement and immobilizes the innumerable animate creatures and inanimate objects that inhabit every page of the book.

Trusting the infallible choice of his inner vision, Cemí chooses two statuettes, a bacchante "gently swaying to the rhythms of the dance," and a Cupid without a bow who, thus disarmed, resembles an angel, "a youth in a Persian miniature" with something as well "of the Greek or Inca athlete following the prodigious Veracocho." He places these objects on his dresser and what happens then associates the initial meditation on words-become-objects with what will happen to these objects that become words in their subtle chain of *similitudes amies* (to quote Valéry again):

> Days before, in his own study, he had studied a cup of solid silver which he had brought from Puebla, beside a Chinese buck worked out of a single piece of wood. At his side, by itself on another table, a fan disquieted the buck (more than is natural for such animals) as he drew near the silver cup, his fear ancestral, cosmological, of the hour of watering, after running through the grazing lands. The buck, frightened because he saw a sudden storm wind rise, no longer stood beside the cup in his usual pleasant pose, his skin trembled, as when he felt the gust passing over the grass, the serpent's fumes on the protective cloak of the dew.
>
> To give the wooden buck peace, not only had the cup to be moved away, but the fan had to be turned off. Cemí lifted the Pueblan cup to the upper reaches of the little cabinet, setting it between the angel and the bacchante. He realized that the chaotic tastelessness of the show window at Obispo calmed itself in the polished mahogany that topped

the cabinet, when he set the cup between the two bronze statuettes. The angel appeared to run and jump without dizzying himself along the circle of the cup's lip, and the bacchante, exhausted from striking her cymbals and making gaudy leaps, collapsed at the foot of the cup, from where the angel resolved to retrieve her for the games of the round light at the cup's lip. (357)

The final step is metaphysical; it is the axis around which the system that makes *Paradiso* possible crystallizes, a system that uses the image to make visible the world of essences we can usually visit only momentarily. But then Cemí notices that the serene pleasure these groupings bring him, "where a field of force succeeds in establishing itself in the center of the composition," provokes in others "a cross and even confused reaction, as if of supreme mistrust." The imaginary cities he has seen rise up in the conciliation and harmony of the rhythms provoke angry gestures in those who remain outside an architecture at once intuited and set into operation by the spirit. In a passage that has the "dark clarity" of Corneille's famous line, Lezama crowns his vision:

> That brought him to meditate on the manner in which those spatial
> rearrangements were produced in him, that ordering of the invisible,
> that feeling for stalactites. He was able to establish that those group-
> ings had temporal roots, had nothing to do with spatial groupings,
> which are always a still life; for the viewer, the flow of time converted
> those spatial cities into figures, through which time, as it passed back
> and forth like the labor of the tides on the coral reefs, produced a kind
> of eternal change of the figures, which by being situated in the distance
> were a permanent embryo. The essence of time, which is the ungrasp-
> able, by its own movement that expresses all distance, achieves the
> reconstruction of those Tibetan cities which enjoy all mirages, the
> quartz doe of the contemplative way, but into which we are not able
> to penetrate, for a time in which all animals begin to speak has not

been bestowed on man, everything external producing an irradiation which reduces him to a diamond essence lacking walls. The man knows that he cannot penetrate into those cities, but in him there is a disquieting fascination with those images, which are the only reality that comes toward us, that bites us, a leech that bites without a mouth, that by a completive method sustains the image, like most of Egyptian painting, and wounds us precisely with what it lacks. (358)

In our mooring at Lezama I have assumed that the reader does not know *Paradiso,* which, like so many other Cuban books and indeed all of Cuba, is still waiting for the rest of Latin America to decide to confront its true destiny. That is why I hasten to clear up the misunderstanding that would result from assuming that the whole book is in the tone of the passages I have quoted. These passages offer some keys to the novel, but it actually operates on many levels, from everyday domestic descriptions to extreme erotic, magical, and imaginary situations. It is impossible to convey the multiplicity of connected or free episodes, the sequential and cross-referential scenes, the inexhaustible fantasy of a man who uses the image as a fabulous falconry in which the falconer, the falcon, and the capture triangulate a primary series of reactions that multiply into a vast crystal containing an entire world, a "Tibetan city" of absolute enchantment. I offer an example that I hope will provide a sense of the lifeblood that runs through *Paradiso,* the human presence that hypostatizes all that is Cuban and American, the arduous proposition of recording height and length, above and below, myth and folklore, and at the same time letting us in on games and table talk, longing for absent loves, empty opera halls, and the Havana waterfront at daybreak after an endless walk. So:

José Cemí remembered the Aladdin-like days when Grandmother would get up in the morning and say, "Today I feel like making a pudding, not the kind they eat these days, which is like restaurant food, but something closer to a custard or a thick pudding." Then the whole house was at the old lady's disposal. Even the Colonel obeyed her, imposing a religious submission, as with a queen once regnant who years later, when her son the king was obliged to visit armories in Liverpool or Amsterdam, reassumed her old prerogatives and heard once more the whispered flattery of her retired servants. She asked what boat had brought the cinnamon, then held it aloft by the root for a long time and ran the tips of her fingers over the surface, the way one tests the antiquity of a parchment, not by the date of the work hidden in it but by the width, by the boldness of the boar's tooth that engraved the surface. She lingered even more over the vanilla, not pouring it directly from the bottle, but with drops soaking her handkerchief, and afterwards, in irreversible cycles of time that only she could measure, she went on sniffing until the message from that dizzying essence faded away, and only then would she pronounce it worthy of participation in a dessert mixed by her; or else she poured the bottle's contents into the grass in the garden, declaring it harsh and unusable, obeying, I think, some secret principle to destroy whatever was deficient and unfulfilled, so that those who settle for little would not come across the rejected matter and preserve it. She reestablished herself with loving domination, a trait whose ultimate refinement was its obvious balance, and said to the Colonel, "Get the irons ready to singe the meringue, because soon we'll paint a mustache on Mont Blanc," voiced with an almost invisible laugh, intimating that the creation of a dessert elevated the house toward the supreme essence. "Now don't beat eggs in milk. Mix the two after you beat them separately; each should grow in itself, and then you put together what they've blossomed into." The sum total of these delicacies would be put on the fire as Doña Augusta, watching it boil, saw it form into the yellow ceramic-like pieces, served on plates with a dark red surface, a red that came out of night. Then Grandmother passed from her nervous commands to an impassive indifference. There was no need for praise, hyperbole, encouraging love pats, importunate reiteration of its sweetness. Nothing seemed to matter to her any more and she took up talking to her daughter again. Now she seemed to be asleep, while her daughter was telling her something. Or she was mending socks, while the other was talking. They would change rooms, one as if she were looking for something she remembered at that moment, leading the other by the hand, talking, laughing, whispering. (12–13)

Thus we learn of the death of Andresito and of Eloisa, and of the marriages of José Eugenio, with the delicious episode of the boots of his sweetheart Rialta, mother of José Cemí and the most enchanting feminine figure in the book; the disappearance of José Eugenio brings the life of his son to the forefront, and from him and with him we get to know Demetrious and Blanquita and are present at the marvelous game of chess when Uncle Alberto reads mysterious messages hidden inside the jade pieces, creating a magical atmosphere, until José Cemí secretly discovers that the little pieces of paper were actually blank and that the magic was even heavier for being imaginary and poetic. The phallic rituals of Leregas and Farraluque have something of an aping parody anticipating the extraordinary debate on homosexuality that reveals the character of Fronesis and Foción at the same time that it defines a mythic and poetic anthropology. The chapters that lead to the end of the work are the most novelistic in regard to narrative and character: the drama of Foción before Fronesis, the bitterly humorous story of Fronesis's father and Sergei Diaghilev, culminating in the hallucinatory episode of Foción's madness. This is a poor summation of a novel that will not tolerate summarizing, that demands a *literal* reading, but in the meantime it would be selfish to resist the urge to cite twists, discoveries, and jests like these:

> The olive green of his uniform contrasted with the yolk-like yellow of the melon; when he shifted it to relieve its fatiguing weight, the melon took on the vital appearance of a dog. (14)

Andresito, Doña Augusta's eldest son, before shaking the sweat several times from the bow of his violin, would begin to fold the pages of his score, and with that silence of a stout commodore before the first notes . . . (40)

The President crossed the ballroom like a nicety on the lid of a cigar box. (105)

On waking, he sensed the undefined collection of silences that surround a tiger, a silence lying in wait, unfolding under the tiger's auditory captation. (229)

It caused the sensation of being a transmuter of hours, it bore the secret of the metamorphoses of time, the hours inhabited by a dormouse or a terrapin, it transformed them into the hours of a falcon or a cat with electrified whiskers. (327)

They'll consider him a victim of high culture, like those victims in detective stories who prefer to enter their houses through the window. (429)

The house, the candles in their holders, seemed to stress its metals, as if preparing the fireflies of memory for the future. (119)

Once Uncle Alberto, arguing with his mother, Doña Augusta, broke a Sèvres tureen with pastoral scenes, the goats left with just one jawbone, a pair of short pants left without a leg in the morning rehearsal of courtly dances. Doña Augusta continued her contralto imprecations, refusing to sell her last shares of Western Union; then the French cut-crystal ashtray, jumping like a quartz mine under the puffing and mad running of gnomes, deposited its fragments in the woven wicker basket. (77–78)

Its owner was Colonel-of-Independence Castillo Dimás, who spent three months on the plantation during the harvesting and grinding season, three months on some keys he owned near Cabañas, a completely Eden-like locale, where he slept like a gull, ate like a shark, and bored himself like a marmot in the Para-Nirvana. (213)

Then he caught up with a former mistress, Hortense Schneider, an Isoldic and light-fingered Prussian beauty, then in her diminishing forties, with circles under her eyes and lips as communicative as the pines of the Rhine. Growing old in such a Wagnerian way, in her immoderate concept of grandeur, she had switched continents, and now in China she went on playing her Isoldic role, restricting herself to being the emperor's mistress. (441)

Paradiso is like the sea, and the preceding quotes suffer the sad fate of any medusa detached from its green belly. Surprised at first, now I understand the gesture my hand makes to reach out and turn the pages of this huge volume one more time; this is not a book to read in the way that one reads books, it is an object with obverse and reverse, weight and density, smell and taste, a center of vibration you will never succeed in knowing intimately unless you approach it with a certain amount of tact, seeking the entrance through osmosis and sympathetic magic. How admirable that Cuba has given us two great writers who defend the baroque as the code and emblem of Latin America, and that their work possesses such a richness that Alejo Carpentier and José Lezama Lima could be the two poles of the vision and manifestation of the baroque, Carpentier the impeccable novelist of European technique and lucidity, the author of literary works without a trace of innocence, maker of books refined to the tastes of that Western specialist, the reader of novels; and Lezama Lima, intercessor in the dark operations of the spirit that precedes the intellect, of those zones that provide pleasure we don't understand, of the touch that hears, the lips that see, the skin that perceives the flutes at the Pannic hour and the terror of crossing streets under the full moon. In its highest moments, *Paradiso* is a ceremony, something that surpasses all readings with literary ends and modes in mind; it has that zealous presence typical of the primordial vision of the Eleatics, amalgam of what would later be called poem and philosophy, naked confrontation between man's face and a sky full of columns of stars. A work like this isn't *read;* it is consulted, you move through it line by line, essence by essence, with an intellectual and sensory involvement as tense and deeply felt as that contained in these lines and essences, which seem to reach out to us and expose us. Pity the poor soul who tries to travel through *Paradiso* the way you go through "the book of the month," that television show on the pages of ordinary novels. Since my first encounter with the poetry of Lezama I have known that this *Paradiso* would be the crowning of an imperial work. And therefore, as to reach Montego Bay,

> después que en las arenas, sedosas pausas intermedias,
> entre lo irreal sugerido y el denso, irrechazable aparecido,
> se hizo el acuario métrico, y el ombligo terrenal
> superó el vicioso horizonte que confundía al hombre con la
>   reproducción de los árboles,

we must remember the myth of the Idumeans, who reproduced vegetatively, without "ombligo terrenal," without time, "acuario métrico," so, in the same way, every dark and risky page of *Paradiso,* every uprooting or estranging image, requires a humble but profound love of the first morning discovered in the garden of Eden, a deciphering of herbs, seclusions, and comportments, a ritual cadence that in the middle of the trance and enchantment opens the doors of a great mystery that is resolved in the brilliance of this masterwork. Thanks to *Paradiso* — as in their day one thanked *Loco Solus* or *The Death of Virgil* — I return to the written word in the spirit of a child who slowly passes a finger over the maps in the atlas, over the contours of the images, who savors the inebriating pleasures of the incomprehensible, of words that are incantations, rhythms, and rites of passage: "Before the calends of July . . . Fifteen men on the coffin of the dead . . . They departed for the conquest of the Tower of Gold . . . Open, Sesame . . . The monsoons and the trade winds . . . Don't forget that we owe Esculapio a cock . . ." These days we weigh the dead albatross, we have become wise, but the fundamental attitude remains the same, because it is that of all poets who seek or transmit a participation in the essential. *Paradiso* can be read in the manner of Orphic hymns, or bestiaries, or *Il Milione* by the Venetian, or Paracelsus, or Sir John Mandeville, and in the oracle's cadenced consultation, where a certainty palpitates that transcends enigmas, the absurdity and incredulity of intellectual technique, the reader passes into the verb and through the verb to a transcendent encounter, he is before the entrails the soothsayer reads, before the mantic tablets, the signs of the I Ching and the *libris fulguralis*. To read *Paradiso* this way is to look at the fire in the fireplace and enter into its whirlwind of creation and annihilation, its classical moment in which it is the sacrificial fire, its romantic hour full of sparks and unexpected explosions, its baroque of blue and green smoke that multiplies ephemeral statues and cornucopias, its Aura Mazda instant, its Brunhilda instant, the cosmic sign of Empedocles, the spiral turns of Isadora Duncan, the analytic sign of Bachelard, and, underneath, always, the old women of the hyperborean coasts who read in the flames the fate of those on the high seas who confront the Kraken and the unchained leviathan. Man has reached the moon, but twenty centuries ago a poet knew the enchantments that would make the moon come down to earth. Ultimately, what is the difference?

· TC ·

LETTER FROM LEZAMA (1969)

SEVERO SARDUY

Sr. Severo Sarduy   21 July 1969
In Paris

Dear friend:

I have received your words which summon me to the feast of the baroque pineapple of Sceaux, pictured in your lovely illustration. Every trip is highly problematic for me, however; since I did not acquire the habit of traveling in my youth, now that I've reached maturity, every translocation takes on a hysterical pace characterized by banal worries, manias, and annoyances. At this point hopping about holds little attraction for me, and in truth what I would like to do is spend a year in Paris or Madrid, resting and recuperating, because in recent years my health, although not precarious, has been unstable. If I could make the trip with my wife, I think everything would move along at a nice andantino pace. Everything strikes me as confusion, as clouds galloping, but then the ray of grace begins its work, and the day eventually takes shape. You, no doubt, will understand my moods quite well.

Back to our dear bits of flesh. You ask my opinion about whether the book should appear in one volume or two. It would not displease me if both *were to appear in bookstores at the same moment,* although I would prefer a single volume, because if a space of time, however brief, were to intervene between the first volume and the second, the unity of the work would suffer from that delay. Any interval would open a lacuna in the center of the work. I also realize that the publisher's reasons for issuing the work in either one volume or two must have a sound basis. You have shown such affectionate support for *Paradiso* all along — and this has afforded me much happiness — and you will know how to find the right leverage, the best solution.

I'm already enamoored of the volume of Baudelaire's collected works that you people are about to publish. I await this gift, which all by itself will occasion an Easter or a christening. One of Baudelaire's most significant assertions is like a prism, and I turn it often: "What makes the world revolve is nothing but universal misunderstanding; through misunderstanding the whole world reaches agreement. Because, unfortunately, if everyone were to understand each other, no one would ever get along."

How true of our own times: if it weren't for alienation, contemporary life could not achieve its logos. If alienation were to be suppressed, life would become a plain of snow, in the same way that Saint Augustine called early for the existence of heretics and, much later, Gracián accepted with tolerant bitterness that "this world creates harmony from disharmony." That's why Baudelaire had to seek help from the devil of lucidity, a kind of alienation.

Affectionately,
J. Lezama Lima

"THE BAROQUE PINEAPPLE OF SCEAUX" is more the product of local confectionery than a Lezamesque metaphor for my letter of invitation: Seuil, where *Paradiso* was being published in the series that I currently inspire, had invited Lezama to Paris to celebrate the appearance of the book. In the still life formed by Lezama's writing, carefully perfected and asymmetrical like a Spanish still life — although in it the delicacies and fruits of the Peninsula have been replaced by Cuba's sizzling cornucopia, and okra, *caimitos,* guavas, and mangoes blur the precise, attenuated geometry of apples — what prevails is a "glazed" or candied nature. Syrup, that artless alchemy of the nation's sugar, provides a perfect finish and frosts everything, packing fruits and pastries into a saccharine layer of topping, which in the heat and over time becomes cloudy and thickens like heavy glass. This cloying quality, however, is nothing but the stamp of a vaster conquest or appropriation, in which Lezama acknowledges the spirit of Cuba's Mambí patriots, the signs of their insurrection, an inkling of subversion: ". . . the arrogance of Spanish cuisine as well as the sensuality and surprises of Cuban cuisine, which may seem Spanish but declared its independence in 1868."[1]

I am not forgetting the actual iced fruits in question, bursting with their own unadulterated juices in barely thickened fillings and adorned with their own crowns; along with the small, still bloody trophies from forest hunts, they brighten the streets of Sceaux and renew in some way the festive baroque tradition of the Castle, which Colbert

1. *Paradiso* (Mexico: Era, 1968), 17. (*Paradiso,* trans. Gregory Rabassa [Austin: University of Texas Press, 1974], 15. [Translation somewhat modified here. (Trans. note.)])

entrusted to Claude Perrault, and which Le Brun, with the help of Coysevox and Girardon, would temper with his blazing chariots of Dawn and ceiling decorations insistent in their monarchical metaphors. Racine's *Phaedre,* to which Lezama refers constantly, was performed at the inauguration; later, for a visit of the sovereign and Madame de Maintenon, the court poet composed an "Idyll of Sceaux," a celebration devoted to the victories of the Sun King.

The banquet I attempted to offer the master[2] was enameled, then, by both the gastronomical marvels from areas around Paris and the textual connotations of a time — the classicism of metrical rigor, the baroque of the Racinian image — that in Lezama achieved the category of *era,* those periods of men's imagination when great poetry is lived plentifully.[3]

"SINCE I DID NOT ACQUIRE THE HABIT OF TRAVELING IN MY YOUTH."
Lezama's life is marked by something that was also the center of his poetic system and the title of his key work: *La fijeza* [fixedness]. What

2. Referred to in "Página sobre Lezama" [Page about Lezama], which, along with the manuscript of a letter to his sister Eloísa, forms the back cover of his *Cartas (1939–1976)* [Letters] (Madrid: Orígenes, 1979). The letter I discuss here is not included in that volume and is unpublished.

3. Although the presence of the French classics, among them Racine himself, means that this period cannot be included among Lezama's *eras imaginarias* [imaginary eras] if we adhere to the strict definition of that term: ". . . the conviction that in imaginary eras, in historical periods, the image was expressed so frequently *that even though they did not provide great poets,* poetry was lived fully. No great poets appear between Virgil and Dante; nevertheless it is a time of great poetry. This is the period of the Merovingians when all of Europe fills with exorcisms and wondrous occurrences. The common man is convinced that, like the men of the Old Testament, Charlemagne conquered Zaragoza when he was two hundred and twenty years old, and people set out on pilgrimages and constructed the great stone symbols." *La imagen como fundamento poético del mundo,* by Loló de la Torriente, in *Bohemia,* about 1960(?). Emphasis added.

is more, confinement, a persistent immobility, a phobia of all displacement: "Every translocation takes on a hysterical pace." The "everything" that strikes him "as confusion, as clouds galloping" is the strident set from an opera, or the possibility of moving, the *potens* — to use his term — of the drift, as if the body were *fixed* by genetically inflexible tethers to a familiar city, a circle halfway between the legendary house of the mother and the "unmentionable fiesta" of the island where he was born.

Lezama's biographers make no mention of trips. Armando Alvarez Bravo points out, however, a short stay in Mexico when Lezama, in contact "with the mainland, with the American landscape, enlarged his ideas about this cosmos, of which he knew only one aspect, the islands." Then in 1950 he "takes another, short trip, this time to Jamaica. Basing himself on this trip and on his previous journey, he begins to forge a theory about 'American expression.'"[4] I think that from then on — unless Eloísa Lezama Lima has another version of this — the intimidating area, the region hostile to all displacement narrows gradually, reducing the safeguarded territory that the Mother buoys as she goes about her daily tasks, marking it with her care, as if Lezama's respiratory difficulties prevented him from moving too far from the cadence of that other breath, from an ideal rhythm of contact with space and air, guarantee of both survival and serenity.

In poems like *El arco invisible de Viñales* (The invisible arch of Viñales) he left proof of his travels by interrupting the pure phonetic enjoyment occasioned by his poetry with details so realistic and

---

4. *Lezama Lima, los grandes todos* (Montevideo: Arca, 1968), introduction and interviews by Armando Alvarez Bravo.

minute that they eventually form something like a narrative — the boy selling stalactites, the bottle full of fireflies where he saves the ten céntimos he earns for each stone and which he places under his pillow; his brother, a Picassoist juggler; his mother fanning the door to shoo away a lizard; his sister tiptoeing by so as not to wake anyone, sneaking off to meet her soldier: a vignette that portrays the Cuban peasant family in a way reminiscent of the vignettes of Abela or Victor Manuel. Lezama was not even an island traveler — like those in my own family — addicted to train number 1, which covered Cuba's six provinces at laughable or outlandish speeds, making local stops that filled the platforms to overflowing.

It's true that he went frequently to Bauta, near Havana, the parish of Angel Gaztelu, a priest who was a member of the editorial board of *Orígenes*,[5] to attend Sunday banquets that were Creole anthologies of after-dinner conversations marked by siesta-time sonnets, and also to the weddings and christenings of his friends, faithful, like the rhythm of the seasons, to the cyclic return of Christian commemorations and rituals.[6]

Nevertheless, the sensuality of knowing, the huge number of similitudes, connections, and references this immobile man threads together is so great that as early as the 1930s it amazes the first travelers with whom he discusses his island theology and outlines the bases of his poetic system, which begins with the image as the foundation of the world. Among these travelers were Juan Ramón Jiménez —

5. As evoked, and with the precision only possible for another member of *Orígenes,* by Lorenzo García Vega in *Los años de Orígenes* [The *Orígenes* years] (Caracas: Monte Avila, 1979).

6. In this same letter, Lezama evokes "an Easter or a christening," when he offers the metaphor of the happiness it would cause him to receive the complete works of Baudelaire.

"Lezama, my friend, you are so sharp, so enthusiastic, so vibrant, one can keep talking about poetry with you forever"; María Zambrano, who was then writing her *Cuba secreta,* a veritable decalogue of *Orígenes;* Doctor Pittaluga, of whom Lezama utters what the condescending succession of travelers invited by the revolution will later coin as the image of Lezama himself — "He was a gentleman and he was learned. . . . He was a style personified, he knew how to quote a classic or smoke a cigar with incomparable form"; Luis Cernuda, Wallace Stevens, Karl Vossler. . . .

As if his supreme agility and the brilliance of his associations corresponded, through a law of opposites, to physical fixedness and a confinement both domestic and Cuban, Lezama's culture encompassed, with the lion's glance that is one of the Buddha's attributes at birth, *everything, at the same time.* One simple page can string together, as in a semantic mirage, an improvised, asymmetrical Pythagoreanism; Le Corbusier; a German chest covered with baroque reliefs; one of Brueghel's paintings; a majolica wall tile with an Algerian alms box attached; a tambourine; the rococo Louis XV; Quentin La Tour; the Council of Trent; a scarlet quiver; El Greco; Swedenborg; Boehme; Baudry, who painted biscuit porcelain — to note only explicit references, since the scope of his connotations and bifurcations would encompass an encyclopedic totality.

Whenever I found myself in a place described by Lezama, I always *recognized it from his description* — so precise is what could very well be called his *clairvoyance;* a Tibetan monastery in the Himalayas; the faded green expanse of the Ceylonese rice fields; a head of Saint Anthony from the Museum of the Hot Springs; or the rose window of Notre Dame adjacent to the horizon line of the river. An entire metaphysics of the *right view* — one of Buddhism's guiding principles, according to the first sermon at Sarnath, in which Sakyamuni pointed the way to gazelles and disciples — could be derived from Lezama's visual acuteness, from the way he would spread out and focus his sight before fixing his gaze, as if only the absence and distance of the real object — whose mental mage we contemplate — allowed it to create the impression of reality in the text. An entire science of signs: annihilate, obliterate, scratch out the referent in the distance so that, in the purity and nakedness of the signified, we are granted access to the majesty of the signifier, the concision of the letter. This explains, perhaps, the rigor in Lezama's "fixedness," the almost moral persistence of his immobility, as if things would vanish once they were perceived as literal, as if the rose window of Notre Dame, seen up close, would reduce the incandescence of its ciphers, the ardent ratio of its numbers to "an improvised, asymmetrical Pythagoreanism," as if beyond the *cosa mentale* all things underwent degradation and all that remained of being, which is external to the image, were simulacra or waste products of being.[7]

7. The letter I discuss is dated 21 July 1969. A few days later, Lezama writes to his sister Eloísa, speaking this time about an invitation from UNESCO sent by César Fernández Moreno shortly after the one he received from Seuil; he insists upon the impossibility of any trip and shortens drastically the possible stay he mentions to me. In my letter he says, "What I would like to do is spend a year in Paris or Madrid, resting and recuperating"; in Eloísa's letter he says, "I plan to spend a week in Paris and a month in Madrid."

"As I told you by phone, UNESCO has invited me to Paris to give a talk on Gandhi. I feel so despondent, so indolent and apathetic, that what at other times would have caused me great happiness is the cause of profound worries. To feel alone, without family, without support, can be so enervating that you lose your enthusiasm and decisiveness. María Luisa is encouraging me, and I think that, God willing, we'll make the trip; but these last ten years have been filled with such deep worries, that everything has become problematic and confused for us. If I do make the trip, I plan to spend a week in Paris and a month in Madrid."

To an inquiry about trips from the Centro de Investigaciones Literarias de la Habana [Center for Literary Research of Havana], Lezama answers: "There are

Lezama liked to quote this sentence of Pascal: "It's good to see and not to see, this is precisely the state of nature."

Poetry is *knowledge power.*

"A NICE ANDANTINO PACE." The appearance of this Italian diminutive constitutes an epiphany of the Cuban language. None of the versions of Spanish that have arisen in the Americas have been more devoted to the minuscule, the diminutive, as if twisted or miniaturized words lent themselves immediately to a complete survey of listening: the sonorous surroundings of a Japanese garden. Affection — the most Cuban emotion — borders on the drive to make smaller; reduction amuses and fascinates, brings closer. Cubans have always had an innate aversion to the monumental, which is manifested at the first opportunity by their *choteo,* that useless practical joke or mockery, that irruption of the parodic and slightly grotesque. How many sentences filled with stale oratory or foggy, vulgar lyricism have been ridiculed by a *trompetilla,* the Cuban version of a Bronx cheer, as if they were confronted with their sinister doubles, with their pretentiously paint-smeared impostures.

----

some truly splendid trips, such as those a man can take from his bedroom to the bathroom along the corridors of his house, or parading through parks and bookstores. Why even consider the various means of transportation? I'm thinking about airplanes, where the travelers can walk only from nose to tail: this is not traveling. Travel is little more than a movement of the imagination. Travel is to recognize, recognize oneself, it is the loss of childhood and the admission of maturity. Goethe and Proust, those men of great diversity, almost never traveled. Their ship was the imago. I am the same; I have almost never left Havana. I acknowledge two reasons: each time I left, my bronchial tubes got worse; in addition, the memory of my father's death has floated at the center of every trip. Gide said that every voyage is a foretaste of death, an anticipation of the end. I don't travel: that's why I return to life." From "Interrogando a Lezama Lima" in *Recopilación de textos sobre José Lezama Lima* (Havana: Casa de las Américas, 1970).

Juan Goytisolo used to point out how, contrary to all other countries throughout history, which have considered their wars — no matter what the damage actually amounted to — as incommensurate catastrophes or apocalyptic prefigurations, Cuba christened one of its wars the "little war." He also stressed the graphic, cartoonish impact of the phrase used to sanction every ruined fortune, shattered reputation, or public derision of a former hero: "His little altar collapsed!"

Listening to these oscillations, one could also read Lezama's page as a score of sudden tiny chords, the twists and reductions caused by the diminutive endings that enamel Cuban language with their fiesta of miniatures, like oiled baroque mechanisms always ready to unfurl their parade of sarcastic dwarves, lifting their feet, jangling their little coin-covered jackets.

"AS CLOUDS GALLOPING, BUT THEN THE RAY OF GRACE BEGINS ITS WORK." Baroque stage settings, the Council of Trent's resplendent pedagogy, which resorted unreservedly to the most efficacious, the most explicitly theatrical means to dazzle the faithful, to gather them in the luminous cone filtered by a Borrominesque skylight; beneath the swirling angels of a ceiling by Pozzo, in a single, ascending, spiral movement. All this to achieve the greatest realism, the greatest palpability: mystery incarnate. All this to convince.

"YOU, NO DOUBT, WILL UNDERSTAND MY MOODS QUITE WELL." If only my life, although without the telos that inspired his, could configure sufficient symmetries, parallelisms, coincidences and complicities with Lezama's life to justify this empathy.

"BACK TO OUR DEAR BITS OF FLESH." Assuming I have deciphered correctly "the actual design drawn by his pen — curly and capricious like the trimming that edges the carnation, his favorite flower — the lines of a handwriting that seemed to need no exclamation or question mark in order to leave signs of an incontestable opening, of a different vehemence."[8] I don't recognize this expression as an idiomatic Cuban phrase or remember having heard it in my childhood. It has the realistic ring, however, of an idiolect. Although we may be dealing with nothing more than a question of precedence, an idiomatic phrase, the anonymous knowledge common to everyone, is only the repetition, the image — coined, minted, and worn out by use — of something that thanks to a slight alteration of standard language was once a poet's discovery. And vice versa.

"ANY INTERVAL WOULD OPEN A LACUNA IN THE CENTER OF THE WORK." A curious premonition, in temporal terms, of what in *Oppiano Licario* will be the formal structure. The whole story revolves around a lacuna, a textual absence, or *Súmula:* a Pythagorean key and gnostic summa of the world, to which we never gain access, and which a cyclone and a dog, equally infernal and inopportune, scatter irretrievably. A blank page, the illegible and lacunal mark of the loss that brings to a halt — or centers — the unfinished sequel to *Paradiso.*[9]

8. Fina García Marruz, "Estación de gloria," in *Recopilación de textos sobre José Lezama Lima,* 270.

9. "In this way, the book that establishes a cosmic relation between the exceptions of nature and those of form — the *Súmula* from which, after he snatches it from the dog, Cemí saves only one poem, configured for us as a blank page, although Lezama may have planned to add it when he finished the novel — is forever erased; equally unfinished is the book that, with *Paradiso,* will bring to a close the effort to found the island on the image, on the generative word. It drifts in the river, a mirror on the water, an endless flow, a scattering of ashes: the erased body of the founders." — Severo Sarduy, "*Oppiano Licario:* the book that could not end," *Vuelta* 18 (May 1978), 32. Also *Point of Contact* (Winter 1981), 123.

"OCCASION AN EASTER OR A CHRISTENING." In addition to the comments above about Lezama's fidelity to the observation of Christian rituals, his sense of celebration at once Catholic and Cuban, it is necessary to remember that José Cemí's fate as a poet is identified with that of Christ as a son. This can be read in the first lines of *Paradiso*. Cemí loses his ability to breathe in front of the family servants, metaphors of the Trinity, and the book proceeds from that arrhythmia to a total recovery of breath: the Hesychastic rhythm of the poetry; he defines his life, beginning with the Mother's devotion, as an incarnation or mystery, and is finally recognized by Oppiano Licario thanks to his initials: J. C.[10]

"WHAT MAKES THE WORLD REVOLVE IS NOTHING BUT UNIVERSAL MISUNDERSTANDING; THROUGH MISUNDERSTANDING THE WHOLE WORLD REACHES AGREEMENT. BECAUSE, UNFORTUNATELY, IF EVERY-ONE WERE TO UNDERSTAND EACH OTHER, NO ONE WOULD EVER GET ALONG." I have not found the exact quote in the same edition of Baudelaire's complete works I sent Lezama. But that paradox gives rise to a reading reactivated in the light of current psychoanalysis. The work's permanence, like the prism Lezama turns in order to assemble a phrase, is nothing more than the possibility, forever renewable, of yet another refraction by the sharp edge. Through the translucent other side, the ray of writing, apparently colorless and unified, will open into the rainbow's spreading beam.

Structured, informative language, with its knots and links, precedes us as a large, falsely efficient Other, as the fragile support of our understanding and communication. If we were to rely on this utili-

10. Julio Ortega, "Aproximaciones a *Paradiso*," *Imagen* 40, supplement (1–15 Jan. 1969), 9–16. Reprinted in *Recopilación de textos sobre José Lezama Lima*.

tarian simulacrum, on its fallacious guarantee, we would never understand each other. Only the faults, defects, omissions, lapses in that code permit the suggestion of the subject, permit a glimpse of true communication to outcrop on the compact, marblelike surface of language. Thus the distracted, absentminded listening of the analyst, who pays no attention to the inopportune jumble of composed discourse, to what the analysand thinks he is saying, but hears, rather, a second discourse, on the threshold of the perceptible, when the first discourse keels, reverses, breaks, vacillates, falls.

"Deep down, Chomsky's ideal speaker-listener is what Lacan refers to elsewhere as the subject-supposed-to-know, the subject supposed to know language completely, the subject supposed to know always what he says, and this unique, unchanging, impeccable individual, about whom one dreams, does not exist. Something would be gained, then, if the scientific consideration of this simple formulation of Lacan, which is a kind of fundamental truth, were to serve as a point of departure. Although this cannot be said quickly, it is a fundamental truth — because *misunderstanding is the essence of communication. The error of a considerable number of sciences that are legitimate sciences, however, is to imagine that a thorough understanding of things forms the essence of communication.*"[11]

"A PLAIN OF SNOW." Among the constants of Cuban poetry, patiently catalogued by Cintio Vitier, one finds a predictable paradox of cold, frost, snow; that is, a constellation of courage and sense metaphorized in a "noncoincidence with reality — a lack of fate, an inadequacy for

11. Jacques-Alain Miller, *Cinco conferencias caraqueñas sobre Lacan* (Caracas: Editorial Ateneo de Caracas, 1980), 42. Emphasis added.

profound human communion, an atmosphere of resentment and bitterness, a hidden life, desertion, desolation."[12]

"SAINT AUGUSTINE CALLED EARLY FOR THE EXISTENCE OF HERETICS." An attitude very Catholic in the splendor of its paradox: sin shapes part of the divine design, which, according to medieval *doxes,* needs shadows to highlight its forms and reliefs. Quoted by Claudel, Saint Augustine utters the *etiam peccata:* even sin serves the glory of God and the redemption of the world. Quoted by Lezama, he seems even more concerned with evil, a possible reminiscence of the heresy that gave rise to his teaching: a Manichaean dualism which makes Evil as active a principle as Good, and sees the struggle between these antagonists in the smallest image of divine manifestation. Like Saint Augustine, who prophesies that Antiquity will end with the taking of Rome, who finds himself alive during the twilight of knowledge, and who even wavers in the face of paganism, Lezama continually alludes to the undertow of barbarism in the disquiet of his final years, as he sees the Catholic society in which he has lived suddenly annihilated: for although he wrote on its margins, *against the current,* that society sustained his language and his faith.

The heresy Saint Augustine requires and rejects is Pelagianism. An ascetic born in Great Britain, Pelagius settled in Rome and attempted a dialogue with Augustine when he passed through Africa in 411. Like many Italian refugees, he continued on to Palestine.

Transforming Christianity into pure morality, the Pelagians maintained that man's essential task was to seek virtue, and that he could attain it — since evil in itself does not exist — thanks to his own free

12. Cintio Vitier, *Lo cubano en la poesía* (Universidad Central de las Villas, 1958), 486.

will. They went so far as to concede such minimal importance to original sin that they postulated the futility of baptism. Saint Augustine asserted the contrary, that man cannot save himself without God's intervention, without grace. Perhaps this explains why, centuries later, the members of Port Royal invoked him against the Jesuits. The disciples there did not believe, as did the Manichaeans, in an absolute evil that man should battle with complete devotion. But they did not differ radically from the Manichaeans, maintaining that evil was so strong, man could free himself from it only through grace.

One could weave a probable history of the West starting from this controversy. Until that time, Christianity, like the thought of Antiquity, sustained itself with externals, laws, principles, and obedience. From the moment grace intervenes, one poses questions about the ultimate source of all possible action: the I, the subject, or the external force of grace. Here begins the vast, torturous history of interiority.

One line of thought in the Middle Ages, and in Descartes, then, derived from Saint Augustine. Saint Thomas, on the other hand, subscribed to a return and recovery of Antiquity; whence, explicitly, arose the *Ulysses* and *Paradiso*.[13]

"THIS WORLD CREATES HARMONY FROM DISHARMONY." This famous phrase from Gracián's *El criticón* [The carper] closes the triad that Lezama sketches, for which he provides the background by joining the most distant and apparently dissimilar things in the ray of oblique knowledge. *Trivium* of alienation: around Lezama, from the time of his letter and even until his death, everything will seem like simula-

13. Henri Marrou, "Le pélagianisme," Jean Danielou and Henri Marrou, *Nouvelle histoire de l'eglise*, I, *Des origines à Grégoire le Grand* (Paris: Seuil, 1963), 450–59.

tion and soft laughter, a discreet, general farce. Thanks to the collective consensus of appearance, to the misunderstanding and disorder promulgated in an almost carnivalesque manner, as well as to the category of truth, to inflated, vacuous discourse accepted as a norm and a moral code, the society of the simulacrum functions, survives, even prospers, as if in that fall man were contemplating an indolent telos-free image of his history, a manifestation — grotesque but as valid as any other — of his *potential.*

"THAT'S WHY BAUDELAIRE HAD TO SEEK HELP FROM THE DEVIL OF LUCIDITY, A KIND OF [EMBODIMENT?] OF ALIENATION." I cannot quite decipher the word that follows *kind of;* it might be "embodiment," but the first stroke and the one after the letter *d* are debatable. I prefer, in any case, that this reading of Lezama end by calling, from the place of absence, as in *Oppiano Licario,* upon the reader's concurrence and complicity. The text thrives beyond death, although this may be in the uncertainty of the letter, in the theorem of its shadow. "I have only a few years left now before I experience the terrible crash of the beyond. But I have survived everything, and I will also survive death. Heidegger maintains that man is a being made for death; all poets, however, create resurrection, intone a triumphant hurrah in the face of death. If anyone thinks I exaggerate, he will end up trapped by disaster, the devil, and the circles of hell."[14]

· SJL & CM ·

14. *Recopilación de textos sobre José Lezama Lima.*

SELECTED BIBLIOGRAPHY

Aching, Gerard. *The Politics of Spanish American Modernism by Exquisite Design.* New York: Cambridge University Press, 1997.

Bejel, Emilio. *José Lezama Lima: Poeta de la imagen.* Madrid: Huerga y Fierro Editores, 1994.

Centre de Recherches Latino-Americaines. *Coloquio internacional sobre la obra de José Lezama Lima: Poesía.* Madrid: Editorial Fundamentos, 1984.

Cortázar, Julio. *Around the Day in Eighty Worlds.* San Francisco: North Point Press, 1986.

Dario, Rubén. *Poesía.* Caracas: Biblioteca Ayacucho, 1977.

Ferrer, Ada. *Insurgent Cuba: Race, Nation, and Revolution, 1868–1898.* Chapel Hill: University of North Carolina Press, 1999.

García Vega, Lorenzo. *Los años de Orígenes.* Caracas: Monte Avila Editores, 1979.

Heller, Ben. *Assimilation/Generation/Resurrection: Contrapuntal Readings in the Poetry of José Lezama Lima.* Lewisburg, Pa.: Bucknell University Press, 1997.

Henríquez Ureña, Max. *Breve historia del modernismo.* México City: Fondo de Cultura Económica, 1954.

Laddaga, Reinaldo. *Literaturas indigentes y placeres bajos.* Rosario, Arg.: Beatriz Viterbo Editora, 2000.

Lezama Lima, José. *Confluencias: Selección de ensayos.* La Habana: Editorial Letras Cubanas, 1988.

———. *La expresión americana.* México City: Fondo de Cultura Económica, 1993.

————. *Fascinación de la memoria: Textos inéditos de José Lezama Lima*. Madrid: Editorial Letras Cubanas, 1993.

————. *Obras completas*. Vols. 1 and 2. México City: Aguilar, 1977.

————. *Oppiano Licario*. México City: Ediciones Era, 1985.

————. *Paradiso*. Normal, Ill.: Dalkey Archive Press, 2000.

————. *Poesía completa*. Madrid: Alianza Editorial, 1999.

————. *El reino de la imagen*. Caracas: Biblioteca Ayacucho, 1981.

————. *Relatos*. Madrid: Alianza Editorial, 1999.

Olson, Charles. *The Maximus Poems*. Berkeley: University of California Press, 1983.

Pérez, Louis A. *Cuba: Between Reform and Revolution*. New York: Oxford University Press, 1988.

Perlongher, Néstor. *Poemas completos*. Buenos Aires: Seix Barral, 1997.

Ponte, Antonio José. *El libro perdido de los origenistas*. México City: Editorial Aldus, 2002.

Sanchez-Eppler, Benigno. *Habits of Poetry: Habits of Resurrection*. London: Tamesis Books, 1986.

Sarduy, Severo. *Christ on the Rue Jacob*. San Francisco: Mercury House, 1995.

————. *Obra completa*. Buenos Aires: Editorial Sudamericana, 1999.

Simón, Pedro. *Recopilación de textos sobre José Lezama Lima*. Madrid: Casa de las Américas, 1970.

Stein, Gertrude. *Lectures in America*. London: Virago Press, 1988.

Vitier, Cintio. *Lo Cubano en la poesía*. Santa Clara: Universidad Central de las Villas, 1958.

CREDITS

Translations not listed below are published in this volume for the first time.

Thomas Christensen's translation of "To Reach Lezama Lima" originally appeared in Julio Cortázar, *Around the Day in Eighty Worlds* (San Francisco: North Point Press, 1986).

James Irby's translations first appeared in these issues of *Sulfur:* "Ten Prose Poems," no. 3 (1982); "Interview with José Lezama Lima," no. 24 (spring 1989); "Confluencias" (Confluences), no. 25 (fall 1989); "Thoughts in Havana," no. 31 (fall 1992).

Suzanne Jill Levine and Carol Maier's translation of "Letter from Lezama" originally appeared in Severo Sarduy, *Christ on the Rue Jacob* (San Francisco: Mercury House, 1995). Reprinted by permission.

G. J. Racz's translation of "Rhapsody for the Mule" appeared in slightly different form in *Post Road* 4 (2002).

Nathaniel Tarn's translation of "An Obscure Meadow Lures Me" was originally published in *Con Cuba*, ed. Nathaniel Tarn (London: Cape Goliard Press/New York: Richard Grossman Publishers, 1969). © Nathaniel Tarn, 1969.

Robert Tejada's translations of "Insular Night: Invisible Gardens" and "A Bridge, a Remarkable Bridge" first appeared in *Abacus;* his translations of "Surprised," "Unleashed," "The Neck," and "Anthony and Cleopatra" first appeared in *Skanky Possum;* and his translations of "Mother," "They Slip through the Night," "Dissonance," "I Heard a Bird," "Old Surrealist Ballad," and "Pavilion of Nothingness" first appeared in *Sulfur*. "A Bridge, a Remarkable Bridge" and "Old Surrealist Ballad" also appeared in *Bomb* (winter 2003–2004). Grateful acknowledgment is made to the editors of those journals.

TEXT: 10.75/15 GRANJON
DISPLAY: AKZIDENZ GROTESK
COMPOSITOR: BOOKMATTERS, BERKELEY